How to Be Happy

According to Jesus

The Beatitudes—Matthew 5:1-12

DR. DAVID JEREMIAH

with Dr. David Jeremiah

© 1996 by Turning Point for God
P.O. Box 3838
San Diego, CA 92163

Published by Walk Thru the Bible Ministries, Atlanta, Georgia.

Unless otherwise indicated, Scripture verses quoted are taken from the NEW KING JAMES VERSION.

Printed in the United States of America.

Contents

About
Dr. David Jeremiah
and Turning Point

D r. David Jeremiah is the founder of Turning Point, a ministry committed to providing Christians with sound Bible teaching relevant to today's changing times through radio broadcasts, audiocassette series, and books. Dr. Jeremiah's "common sense" teaching on topics such as family, stress, the New Age, angels, and biblical prophecy forms the foundation of Turning Point.

Dr. Jeremiah is the senior pastor of Shadow Mountain Community Church in El Cajon near San Diego, California, where he also serves as president of Christian Heritage College. He and his wife, Donna, have four children.

In 1982, Dr. Jeremiah brought the same solid teaching to San Diego television that he shares weekly with his congregation. Shortly thereafter, Turning Point expanded its ministry to radio. Dr. Jeremiah's inspiring messages are currently broadcast weekly from more than 300 national and international radio stations.

Because Dr. Jeremiah desires to know his listening audience, he travels nationwide holding "A Night of Encouragement" radio rallies and Spiritual Enrichment conferences that touch the hearts and lives of many. According to Dr. Jeremiah, "At some point in time, everyone reaches a turning point, and for every person that moment is unique, an experience to hold onto forever. There's so much changing in today's world that sometimes it's difficult to always choose the right path. Turning Point offers real people an understanding of God's Word, as well as the opportunity to make a difference in their lives."

Dr. Jeremiah has authored ten books including *Escape the Coming Night* (Revelation), *The Handwriting on the Wall* (Daniel), *Turning Toward Joy* (Philippians), *Turning Toward Integrity* (James), *Acts of Love: the Power of Encouragement*, *Invasion of Other Gods* (New Age), *Overcoming Loneliness*, and his latest release, *What the Bible Says About Angels*.

About This Study Guide

The purpose of this Turning Point study guide is to reinforce Dr. David Jeremiah's dynamic, in-depth teaching on the Beatitudes and to aid the reader in applying biblical truth to his or her daily life. This study guide is designed to be used in conjunction with Dr. Jeremiah's *How To Be Happy According To Jesus* audiocassette series, but it may also be used by itself for personal or group Bible study.

Structure of the Lessons

Each lesson is based on one of the tapes in the *How To Be Happy According To Jesus* audiocassette series and focuses on passages in the Bible. Each lesson is composed of the following elements:

• Outline

The outline at the beginning of the lesson gives a clear, concise picture of the topic being studied and provides a helpful framework for readers as they listen to Dr. Jeremiah's teaching.

• Overview

The overview summarizes Dr. Jeremiah's teaching on the topic being studied in the lesson. Readers should refer to their own Bibles as they study the overview.

• Application

This section contains a variety of questions designed to help readers dig deeper into the lesson and the Scriptures and to apply the lesson to their daily lives. For Bible study groups or Sunday school classes, these questions will provide a springboard for group discussion and interaction.

• Did You Know?

This section presents a fun fact, historical note, or insight which adds a point of interest to the preceding lesson.

Using This Guide for Group Study

The lessons in this study guide are suitable for Sunday school classes, small group studies, elective Bible studies, or home Bible study groups. Each person in the group should have his or her own study guide.

When possible, the study guide should be used with the corresponding tape series. You may wish to assign the study guide as homework prior to the meeting and then use the meeting time to listen to the tape and discuss the lesson.

For Continuing Study

A complete catalog of Dr. Jeremiah's materials for personal and group study is available through Turning Point. To obtain a catalog, additional study guides, or more information about Turning Point, call 1-800-947-1993 or write to: Turning Point, P.O. Box 3838, San Diego, CA 92163.

Dr. Jeremiah's "Turning Point" radio broadcast is currently heard on more than 300 national and international radio stations. Contact your local Christian radio station or Turning Point for program times in your area.

How to Be Happy
According to Jesus

The Beatitudes—Matthew 5:1-12

INTRODUCTION

Bill Borden was born into a wealthy, aristocratic family in the Northeast. His family owned several industrial concerns, and it was always assumed that one day Bill would take over the family empire from his father. But while he was studying at Yale, the Lord got hold of Bill's life. He started reading his Bible in a fresh way, and thought about Christ's call for Christians to spread the Good News to all people. He went one semester and announced that he was going to be a missionary to China.

Bill's parents couldn't believe what they were hearing. They had all the money, power, and prestige most people only dream about, and their son wanted to give up all those advantages to live in a shack in China! His father told him that he was to stay and run the businesses. If he left for China, he would be disinherited. All the money and prestige would be taken away from him. But Bill Borden left for China anyway. Just a few months after he arrived, he took sick and died. As they were cleaning out his room, his friends found a note on his desk. The note read simply, 'No retreat. No return. No regrets.'

Bill Borden knew something that most people in our world don't discover until it's too late: the world's values won't make you happy. Our world and its system claim that, to be happy, you need to be successful. It says that money and possessions will make you happy, that great accomplishments and fame will give you inner joy and satisfaction, and pleasure will make life worth living. Our culture values pride, power, and possessions. If you do something great, make sure everybody knows about it. Cover up mistakes and pain, the world says, because they'll make you appear weak. Drive yourself to succeed, climb the corporate ladder, and live the American Dream—those are the things that will bring joy to your life. Satisfy your longings and desires, for physical pleasure is what we are all striving for. Happiness can be found in unrestrained sensual freedom. And if anybody tries to stop you, push them out of the way. But Bill Borden rejected that philosophy. He had discovered that all the money, fame, and power in this world will never satisfy; that Satan has deceived mankind into thinking happiness can be bought. Borden knew that happiness isn't found in getting, but in giving.

In the Sermon on the Mount, Jesus offered a plan for happiness that was entirely at odds with the world's perspective. Rather than focusing on pride, the Lord recommended being humble. Rather than pushing for pleasure or possessions, Christ said true joy is found in those who help others, seek God, and feel sorrow for their sin. Instead of pushing others out of the way, Jesus tells us to minister to them. His prescription for happiness is exactly the opposite of the world's.

The Beatitudes are some of the most remarkable pronouncements Christ ever made, and they provide a plan for finding real happiness in an unhappy world. Everyone seems to be seeking happiness, but few seem to find it. In a world that never seems to deliver happiness to those looking for it, Jesus offers a path to true joy. So come and examine His pronouncements—find out how you can experience deep joy in the Lord.

LIFE OUTSIDE THE AMUSEMENT PARK

Matthew 5:1-12

A study of the Beatitudes reveals the true path to happiness.

OUTLINE

Everyone is seeking happiness, but most people never find it. In the Sermon on the Mount, Jesus explains to us what true happiness is and how we can find it.

- I. The Pursuit of True Happiness Is Part of God's Purpose for You and Me
- II. The Pursuit of True Happiness Is a Journey Inward
- III. The Pursuit of True Happiness Is not a Goal but a By-Product
- IV. The Pursuit of True Happiness Will Lead You Ultimately to Jesus Christ

An Englishman once said, "The trouble with you Americans is that you have to be so confoundly happy. You have dedicated yourselves to the pursuit of happiness. And you boast about it as an inalienable right, as though happiness were the supreme and absolute goal of all existence. Surely there are more important things in life than just to be happy."

Happiness is an American right. It's in our Declaration of Independence, right alongside life and liberty. I know people living within that truth of the Declaration of Independence, their whole life wrapped up in the pursuit of happiness. Sometimes it can be confusing to watch them. One man buys a dozen homes in hopes of making himself happy; another goes into the wilderness to live like a hermit. One woman becomes a nun in hopes of finding happiness, another a harlot. One young man thinks happiness is found in body building, while another tries to find it by destroying his body with drugs. One couple thinks happiness is found in children, while another couple is convinced children get in the way of happiness.

Malcolm Muggeridge once called the pursuit of happiness the most disastrous purpose set before mankind, something slipped into the Declaration after "life and liberty" at the last moment, almost by accident. "Happiness is like a young deer," Muggeridge said, "fleet and beautiful. Hunt him, and he becomes a poor frantic quarry; after the kill, just a piece of stinking flesh." In his *Screwtape Letters*, C.S. Lewis had the arch-devil, Screwtape, advise his apprentice demons on the lure of happiness. He called it "an ever-increasing craving for an ever-diminishing pleasure." That's exactly how the pursuit of happiness works in this world.

In James Houston's book, *In Pursuit of Happiness*, a woman named Gloria describes her pursuit of happiness as being at an amusement park.

> Many times I have felt as if I am trapped on a huge roller coaster that goes up and down, round and round. Sometimes I manage to escape and get off the mad ride, but I'm still in the amusement park. Outside the park the world looks exciting, but it's too risky. I'm not sure that I could survive out there, so the amusement park

remains still the biggest attraction in my life. For everyone is being persuaded to stay inside the gates of the amusement park and get back on the roller coaster . . . Yet I still think of people in the past who have gone outside the park. They are the ones who truly seek God with all their heart, mind, soul, and body, and are fully prepared to give it all up. They are the ones who live uncompromising lives, who don't feel the grip of money, the pressure of society, the weakened desire for goodness, the punctured self-discipline, the crushing fear of the future, the horror of death, the threat of injustice, the need of security, the rule of self. They don't struggle for faith, hope, and love; they pour out from them and through them. It is these people outside the park who seem to be so totally free . . . I am not happy. I wish I could live outside the amusement park. I wish I had the stuff to do it, but I am afraid at the center I am empty.

I know people who live in the amusement park, getting off the roller coaster long enough to gaze through the gates at real life outside, but without the courage to go there. As soon as the roller coaster stops, they get back on. Pleasure is an anesthesia for deadening the pain of their empty lives. There seem to be few happy people around today. That's why I appreciate the words of Jesus in the Sermon on the Mount. Nine different times Jesus uses the word *blessed*, which roughly translates to "happy." The core values Jesus offers in the Beatitudes describe life that is really worth living: life outside the amusement park.

Blessed means "happy, blissful, joyous, ecstatic." In the original Greek, there is no verb in any of the beatitudes. So the verses literally say, "Blessed the meek" and "Blessed the poor in spirit." Those characteristics the Lord lists are like an explosion on His lips, a description of the inner joy we can experience. This expression was commonly seen in the Book of Psalms. "Blessed is the man who walks not in the counsel of the ungodly," it says in Psalm 1:1. Anyone who has ever been burned by ungodly counsel will attest to the fact that a man who doesn't get mixed up with ungodly counsel is happy. "Blessed is he whose transgression is forgiven," we read in Psalm 32:1. We are to be blissful and ecstatic over the fact that the Lord has taken away our sins. That's the same expression Christ used when He began talking about the

Christian life. *Blissful, happy, joyous*—these are the words that describe the Christian walk.

Matthew 5:1-12 describes nine characteristics of the happy Christian life. If you want to know what happiness is all about, search through this "happiness manifesto" from the Lord Jesus. He'll explain to you what true happiness is all about. As you study them carefully, you'll find some surprising truths become clear.

The Pursuit of True Happiness is Part of God's Purpose for You and Me

C.S. Lewis enjoyed telling the story of the child who was asked what he thought God was like. As far as the child could make out, God was always snooping around to see if anyone was enjoying himself, so that He could put a stop to it! Have you ever known anyone like that? There are Christians who act that way—"If you're not sad, you can't be holy." But that's dead wrong. Jesus said in John 10:10 that He came "that they may have life, and that they may have it more abundantly." God's purpose is not to create a joyless existence. Jesus spoke those words to make it clear to us that God wants us to be blessed. It's part of His purpose.

Anyone who sees Jesus in any other light is missing the point of His life. When you read about the winsomeness of Jesus and the way He came eating and drinking, you'll see that the Lord enjoyed life. He enjoyed the banquets and the gathering of friends in homes. He mingled with publicans and sinners and was the kind of man who attracted little children to Himself. He had a sense of humor, too, though many people miss it when they read Scripture. He pictured a man with a plank hanging out of his eye, squinting as he removed a speck of sawdust from the eye of a brother. Those who heard that illustration must have giggled with delight at the verbal picture.

The people who try to paint a picture of Jesus as someone sad or morbid have missed the complete picture. He delighted in things, and He wanted us to be happy. He gave us the beatitudes so we would know how to do it. We all have been touched by legalism, but the people of God should be filled with a radiant joy so contagious it cannot be held in. That is the heart of the Lord for you and me.

The Pursuit of True Happiness is a Journey Inward

Those who are truly happy will fit the criteria of what Christ says in Matthew chapter five. A quick scan of chapter 5, verses 1-2 reveals thoughts that run contrary to our current ideas about happiness. There isn't one single reference by the Lord as to health, work, income, financial security, homes, love, or friends. Christ knew that while these things often accompany happiness, they do not ever produce it. His list completely reverses the standards of the world. "Oh, the bliss of the poor!" says Jesus. "The joy of the persecuted! The exaltation of the hungry and thirsty! The happiness of the sorrowful!" These are contradictions to the world's standards. They are sayings that no man can hear without shock or amazement. They are paradoxes that Jesus used to destroy the foolish illusions that so many of His followers had built up about what would happen when He became king.

His followers wanted dominion and prosperity, and Jesus spoke of poverty and sorrow, cutting right to the heart of the people. The words must have disgusted many who heard them. They were like cold water on the hot enthusiasm that so many had for the kingdom. The people were certain the kingdom was going to make them free and rich, but Jesus said, "That's not what the kingdom is about at all."

The Pursuit of True Happiness is Not a Goal but a By-Product

People who start out with the purpose of trying to become happy very seldom arrive at that place. Happiness sought for its own sake is usually self-defeating. The world is on a lark trying to find new ways to be happy, but all people are really doing is trying to mask the pain temporarily.

I read a quote once from a man who said, "I think I must be the happiest man in the world! I have never met anyone who has had as much fun as I have had." The words were not spoken by a playboy or a globetrotter or an adventurer. They were spoken by a Christian missionary by the name of Frank Laubach, whose life was dedicated to the cultivation of literacy among the backward people of the world. He never went searching for happiness—he just found it as a by-product of his search for something more important. Dr. Laubach described delighted men and women weeping for joy when they discovered how to read. "No other work in the world could possibly have brought me so much happiness," he said. He didn't live with prosperity or worldly success, but he found happiness. True joy is a by-product, not a goal.

The Pursuit of True Happiness Will Lead You Ultimately to Jesus Christ

The fifth chapter of Matthew records the words of Jesus regarding happiness. He was an extremely happy man, and His inner joy no doubt came partly from relationships. He had a group of friends who loved Him, and He was endowed with the ability to speak and to heal. If you have a ministry, you know what great joy can be derived from it. Yet over time, the ministry of Jesus Christ shrank. Fewer people followed Him, until the night of the Last Supper when there were just His twelve disciples close by. Knowing that He was about to die and witness the desertion of even His closest friends, Jesus still was able to tell them, "These things I have spoken to you, that My joy may remain in you, and that your joy may be full" (John 15:11).

Jesus, with everything about to come undone, was still able to tell His disciples that He wanted them to be joyful. Can you imagine a man about to die the most terrible of deaths talking of His joy and gladness? Either He must have been insane, or He had an incredible resource of happiness about which our world knows very little. The verses in Matthew chapter five explain His joy, and His words can change our lives. It may not immediately change the way you outwardly live, but it will help you find the inner peace and happiness that makes it possible to find joy in the midst of trial.

When the business in which you have invested your life savings fails, you can still find joy. When the child in whom you have invested your life turns south instead of north, there will still be gladness. When people begin to reject you and turn against you, you can still find happiness in Him. As we work through this study, may each of us discover the joy of knowing the Lord, having our sins forgiven, and being confident that He has a plan for our lives, and heaven is on the agenda. May we find happiness as we look to the words of Jesus Christ in the Beatitudes.

1. How is your life sometimes like an amusement park?

What are the amusements that attract you?

Why are those things a trap?

What do you think is outside the gates of the amusement park?

2. How would you define "happiness"?

How do you suppose Christ would define it?

What makes you happy?

3. In Matthew 5, Jesus uses the term *blessed*. What does that word mean?

4. What do the following passages reveal about happiness:

Psalm 1

Psalm 18:46

Psalm 28:6-7

Psalm 32:1-2

Psalm 84

Psalm 112

5. Does God want us to be happy? Why or why not?

What does the world say will make you happy?

How is that different from the things Christ says will make you happy?

6. How does our culture make the pursuit of happiness an outward expression?

How can the pursuit of happiness become more of an inward journey?

In your view, should happiness be our goal in life? Why or why not?

The title "Sermon on the Mount" doesn't come from the Bible. The Scriptures simply record that Jesus "went up on a mountain, and when He was seated His disciples came to Him" (Matthew 5:1). The "Sermon on the Mount" label was first applied by Augustine, writing a commentary on Matthew in the fourth century. Augustine wrote in Latin, and the phrase did not appear in English until the Coverdale Bible used it in 1535.

HAPPY ARE THE HUMBLE

Matthew 5:3

In this chapter, we will look at what it really means to be "poor in spirit."

OUTLINE

Our culture says that pride and selfishness lead to happiness. But in the Sermon on the Mount, Jesus says that happiness is a result of humility.

I. **Happy Are the Poor in Spirit, for Theirs Is the Kingdom of Heaven**
   A. Those Who Are Poor in Spirit Will Recognize That They Are Out of Step with the World
   B. Those Who Are Poor in Spirit Will Realize Their Emptiness Apart from God
   C. Those Who Are Poor in Spirit Will Reach Out to Others with a Spirit of Love and Cooperation
   D. Those Who Are Poor in Spirit Will Respond to Life with a Spirit of Gratitude
   E. Those Who Are Poor in Spirit Will Reach Their Highest Joy in Serving

Have you ever noticed how many unhappy people there are in this world? With all the comforts and gadgets of our modern world, we don't seem to have found the key to happiness. Even among Christians, with all the God-given gifts at their disposal, there seems to be a lack of happiness. Peggy Noonan, speechwriter for Presidents Ronald Reagan and George Bush, wrote about our national lack of happiness in her book, *What I Saw at the Revolution.* She mentioned that it is embarrassing to live in the most comfortable time in the history of man and still not be happy. In the 1950's, we all watched Ralph and Alice Kramden get by in a small rented apartment with a table, two chairs, and one bureau standing in front of a faded wall. By the 1990's, the set on "Family Ties" consisted of couches, lamps, VCRs, color TVs, and fancy art on the wall. We have more things than our parents did, but we aren't happy, and we feel defensive about it. The dad in the 1950's worked hard to make ends meet. He might not have been happy, but he wasn't put here to be happy, so the knowledge of his unhappiness didn't weigh on him. In the words of Peggy Noonan, "He looks perhaps to other, more eternal forms of comfort."

But somewhere in the sixties or seventies we started living with the expectation of happiness. People started moving, changing jobs or changing partners in a quest for happiness. As Noonan describes it, "We . . . lost the old knowledge that happiness is over-rated." You see, our forebears understood that this is a short, brutal existence we live here on earth, to be followed by an eternity with the Lord. But our generation has decided that this time on earth is the only existence we'll have, the only chance at happiness. So if we search and don't find happiness, we are left only with despair. Many people have pitted their hopes on what this world can provide, and when things start to go bad they have nothing left to bring them joy and peace.

Jesus, in His greatest sermon, spoke to people brutalized and conquered by the Roman armies. They were subdued, poor, and without hope or expectation, yet the Lord said to them, "Happy are the poor in spirit." How could their miserable lives be described as happy?

Happy Are the Poor in Spirit, for Theirs Is the Kingdom of Heaven

In the first words of this great sermon, Jesus begins to describe a new kingdom. It is not the outward kingdom where most people seek happiness but the inward kingdom of the heart. When He speaks of the "poor in spirit," Jesus is not talking about material poverty but about spiritual pride. He is speaking of the inward attitude of the heart. With nowhere else to turn, the desperate may turn to Jesus, the only One who can offer the deliverance they seek. The poor in spirit have the advantage of being able to cry out to God for help.

A person who is poor in spirit goes begging on the inside. His heart is destitute, and he is begging for God to get to the bottom of his problem. When a person comes to this sense of emptiness, he is on the threshold of happiness through the kingdom of God. Psalm 34:18 says, "The Lord is near to those who have a broken heart, and saves such as have a contrite spirit." David noted that "the sacrifices of God are a broken spirit, a broken and a contrite heart—These, O God, You will not despise" (Psalm 51:17). God identifies with those who beg on the inside.

Jesus once told a story of two men praying in the temple. One, a Pharisee, proudly told God all the wonderful things he had done. The other, a tax collector, humbly beat his breast and muttered, "God, be merciful to me, a sinner!" The Lord told this story to a crowd of people who thought themselves righteous, and He noted that it was the tax collector who went home justified. "For everyone who exalts himself will be humbled, and he who humbles himself will be exalted" (Luke 18:14). That tax collector had money, but in spite of his outward wealth, he had a sense of the bankruptcy of his heart. In his emptiness, he cried out to God for mercy. He was blessed because he found God. The Pharisee couldn't get over his self-righteousness and pride to find God. It was the tax collector who came away joyful and at peace, because he had found the Lord. Happiness is an inward thing, not an outward thing. Blessed are the poor in spirit. I wrestle with that concept, since our culture tries to equate happiness with material wealth, but there are at least five things that are outward signs of the inward heart.

Those Who Are Poor in Spirit Will Recognize That They Are Out of Step with the Ways of the World

When a famous basketball player retired at the peak of his career, the owner of the team spoke of him "living the American Dream. The dream is to reach a point in your life where you don't have to do anything you don't want to do, and can do everything that you want to do." After he retired, the man found he wasn't so great at other things. So now he's back playing basketball again. Whatever he's searching for, he hasn't found it.

In our culture, we have a tendency to think that when we finally have enough money to do anything we want, we'll be happy. But that's not where happiness is found. J.B. Phillips has said that our modern world has created its own beatitudes:

> Happy are the pushers, for they get on in the world.
> Happy are the hard-boiled, for they never let life hurt them.
> Happy are they who complain, for they get their own way in the end.
> Happy are the slave-drivers, for they get results.
> Happy are the knowledgeable, for they know their way around.
> Happy are the troublemakers, for they make people take notice of them.

The person who is poor in spirit is simply out of touch with the ways of the world. There is a tension between walking Christ's way and walking in the way of the world.

Those Who Are Poor in Spirit Will Realize Their Emptiness Apart from God

The person who is poor in spirit doesn't boast of his talents or attainments, because he knows he has nothing except from God. If he is gifted, it's because God gave him much. He is humble about his character, knowing he has nothing for which to be conceited. In his soul are the sins that put Christ on the cross. Those who are poor in spirit are the antithesis of the proud; they recognize their spiritual need. We are empty without God. We are impoverished without His blessing. We do not control our own destiny. If we build our dreams on the material world, at any moment they can be dashed.

When mighty Samson had his hair cut off, his strength was gone. Judges 16:20 tells us that Samson "did not know that the LORD had departed from him." He thought he could defeat the foe as he always had done, but now he was without the strength of the Lord. How sad is a man without power, and sadder still the man without power who doesn't know it. No man is so ignorant as he who knows nothing and knows not that he knows nothing! Perhaps you have had a chance to talk to someone like that recently. They try out their ignorance on you, and their utter lack of knowledge is sad. Samson thought he knew what he was doing, but he was utterly mistaken. He didn't know how poor he really was.

In Luke 12:16-21, the Lord Jesus told the story of a man with mistaken ideas of poverty and riches. In a self-centered soliloquy, the man says, "Soul, you have many goods laid up for many years; take your ease; eat, drink, and be merry." Then God said, "Fool! This night your soul will be required of you." Thinking his earthly riches made him righteous, the man was lost due to his own ignorance. "So is he who lays up treasure for himself, and is not rich toward God," added Jesus. If we lay up treasure in the outward kingdom, and never give attention to the inward kingdom, we'll never find happiness. Happiness is not an outward thing, but an inward thing. That's why Jesus said it's so hard for a rich man to get into heaven. He can't push away the things he owns and learn to depend upon the Lord.

The church at Laodicea was like that. Revelation chapter three tells us that the believers thought they were wealthy and in need of nothing, but God saw that they were actually poor, miserable, wretched, blind, and naked. The tragedy isn't that a person will be without what he needs. The tragedy is that a person will never recognize what he truly needs. No man can buy inner happiness. God alone grants happiness to those who seek Him. A person who doesn't understand that is to be pitied.

Those Who Are Poor in Spirit Will Reach Out to Others with a Spirit of Love and Cooperation

The world tells us to develop a thick skin. "Don't let others get close to you, because if they're close, they can hurt you. Keep people away; emotion is a weakness." That's the spirit of this world. But if you read the New Testament, you'll find the spirit of the Lord says the exact opposite. Jesus wept at the tomb of His friend

Lazarus. He took compassion on the lost crowds. He invested in close friendships with the disciples.

The kingdom of God is completely different from the kingdom of this world. A self-centered person won't notice anyone else; his concern is only for himself. He cannot be sensitive to those around him, for fear their pain may ruin his happiness. But a person who is poor in spirit will look to minister. He will seek out those who are hurting, so that he can heal the lives of others. A person filled up with himself is unable to reach out to others, for he loves only himself. A person who is poor in spirit will reach out to others in love.

Those Who Are Poor in Spirit Will Respond to Life with a Spirit of Gratitude

When the Apostle Paul wrote to the Corinthians, he scolded them for being so proud of their spiritual gifts. They went around full of pride, talking about all the good qualities they had, but Paul's question was simple: "Who gave you those gifts?" God did. Why walk around acting proud, as though your spiritual gifts were somehow earned, when they were simply given by the grace of God? The poor-in-spirit person is humble, thanking God for all things because he recognizes that gifts are given by God out of grace and mercy, not because they are earned. Show me a man who is ungrateful, and I'll show you a man who isn't poor in spirit. Show me a woman who is unthankful, and I'll show you a woman who doesn't understand the first Beatitude.

Those Who Are Poor in Spirit Will Reach Their Highest Joy in Serving

Everybody wanted to lift Jesus up as king, but He simply said, "I did not come to be ministered unto, but to minister." A person who truly wants to be happy will find great joy in serving others. Phillip Yancey, a journalist who has had many opportunities to interview sports and entertainment stars, found that those with the highest profiles never seemed to be happy. They were nearly always unfulfilled, self-doubting, and unhappy. But those who had chosen to give their lives to service had a depth and richness that Yancey envied. The doctors working with outcasts, the missionaries translating the Bible into new languages, and the relief workers who had left high-paying jobs for obscurity and service were the ones who had found fulfillment and satisfaction in their lives. Some would argue that they were "wasting" their talents, but these people had discovered that true happiness is found not in getting what you want, but in giving to others what they need.

Don't search for happiness in the outward kingdom; you won't find it. Jesus said, "Blessed are the poor in spirit, for theirs is the kingdom of heaven." The person who is poor in spirit will experience a joy found only in heaven. He will understand what true happiness is—an inward happiness that God gives to those who call on Him.

APPLICATION

1. How do most people seek happiness in our world?

How has that changed in America during the last forty years?

Why has this search for happiness led so many to despair?

2. As you look over Matthew chapter five, does Christ seem to be speaking about the future kingdom or the here and now?

How is it possible to put Christ's words into practice?

What would your response have been if you had been in the crowd and heard Jesus say these words?

3. What does it mean to be "poor in spirit"?

In what ways does the world emphasize pride over humility?

Why is pride so destructive?

How does the world respond to a person poor in spirit?

4. What do the following verses have to say about being poor in spirit?

Psalm 31:9-14

Psalm 34:18

Psalm 51:17

Isaiah 66:2

5. How does that compare with the teaching on pride in the following passages?

Proverbs 11:2

Proverbs 16:18

Proverbs 29:23

Psalm 138:6

Matthew 23:12

6. Who is the happiest person you know?

What makes that person so happy?

Who is the most unhappy person you know?

What has made that person so unhappy?

7. What lessons regarding pride and humility do you glean from Luke 18:10-14?

How does pride separate us from God?

8. In your experience, do you get more long-lasting happiness from giving or from getting? Why is that?

How can service create happiness?

The place from which Jesus gave the Sermon on the Mount is now called "The Mount of Beatitudes." From its rocky sides, you can see the flat plains of farmers' fields spreading out for miles, eventually giving way to the Sea of Galilee. It could have easily held the great multitudes that followed Jesus in His early ministry.

HAPPY ARE THE HURTING

Matthew 5:4

This chapter looks at those who mourn and how God will comfort them.

OUTLINE

Although we don't like pain, God uses it to move us toward happiness. The Scripture shows that hard times lead us toward true happiness.

I. Happiness Is Discovered When We Sacrifice the Present for the Future

II. Happiness Is Discovered When We Sympathize with Those Around Us Who Suffer

III. Happiness Is Discovered When We Sorrow for Our Own Sin

IV. Happiness Is Discovered When We Suffer the Losses and the Crosses of Life

B lessed are those who mourn, for they shall be comforted."
One of the most astounding truths about our generation is
the belief that happiness and freedom from pain are our
inalienable rights as American Christians. We believe that a man
who manages his life well has the right to live above pain and enjoy
happiness. And yet, deep down inside, we know that only children
believe that pain always goes away. Pain is a part of life, and there is
no guarantee of happiness.

Dr. Joseph Fabry has said that the focus of a man's life is the
pursuit of meaning, not the pursuit of happiness. If we expect everything in life to be pleasurable, we invite frustration. In recent years
we have seen some preachers offer a "positive mental attitude"
philosophy of life, negating the example in Scripture that hurt must
sometimes happen. There has never been an attempt on the part of
the biblical authors to give us a Pollyanna view of life. "Pack up your
troubles in your old kit bag and smile, smile, smile" isn't found in
the Old Testament. Instead, the Bible offers a realistic appraisal of
life in the human realm. Abraham cried when his wife Sarah died.
David mourned over the loss of his son Absalom. Jeremiah, the
"weeping prophet," preached his message of judgment with tears. A
woman came to Jesus and washed His feet with her tears. The Lord
Himself wept at the death of His friend Lazarus. He anguished in
the Garden of Gethsemane, watched Peter weep bitterly over his
denial of Him, and comforted the weeping Mary Magdalene outside the tomb on resurrection morning. Where did we ever get the
idea that there is something foreign about tears in life? Why do we
think that tears are a sign of weakness or that they demonstrate a
lack of faith in God? That's not the message of the Word of God.

There are all sorts of reasons for crying. There are tears of devo-
tion, like Mary shed on Jesus' feet. There are tears of concern, like
the Apostle Paul cried as he preached to the Ephesians. There are
tears of regret, like those shed by the Ephesian leaders as they said
good-bye to Paul. There are tears of anguish, shed by the Lord as
He wrestled over the will of God, and tears of compassion, which
Jesus wept as He gazed at the city of Jerusalem. And of course
there are the tears of sorrow that accompany death and disappoint-
ment in this life. The Bible never asks us to pretend we don't hurt.
It doesn't tell us to pretend sorrow is not real. You cannot make

truth disappear merely by wishing it so. In fact, Psalm 56:8 says that God bottles our tears and keeps them, so special are they to our Heavenly Father. Yet, having said that, I struggle with Christ's teaching that those who mourn shall be happy. How can hurting and happiness be synonymous? What do tears have to do with laughter? There are at least four ways that happiness is discovered through hurting.

Happiness Is Discovered When We Sacrifice the Present for the Future

If a Christian accepts the crosses of life, he or she will ultimately be able to wear the crown. If we choose to live for the world to come, we may meet all kinds of sorrow, but we know that joy awaits us. In the story of Lazarus and Dives, the rich man cried out to Abraham in torment after his death. But he was told that he had received good things in this life, so he had earned punishment in the next life. That's the trade-off we face. We sacrifice present joy for future joy. We can take the easy road now and sacrifice the future, or we can sacrifice and discipline ourselves now so that we experience joy in the future. If we mourn now, we shall laugh later.

Students understand that truth. If they discipline themselves today, do their assignments and keep up to date on their reading, they will do well at the end of the semester. Their sacrifice today will bring joy later. But if they decide to experience their joy now, putting parties ahead of homework, their joy now will result in mourning at the end of the semester when grades are posted. Jesus understood this principle. Happy are the hurting, for they shall be comforted. Happiness is discovered when we sacrifice the present for the future.

Happiness Is Discovered When We Sympathize with Those Around Us Who Suffer

Happiness belongs to those who feel sorrow for fellow men and women. Jesus was often described as a man full of compassion for others. He was constantly reaching out to heal and comfort those in pain. Sorrow is a product of love. As we love others, we hurt for their condition. As our love grows, it draws others into its circle. You can't mourn for someone you don't love. Imagine a man who never mourns. He lives by himself, having lost touch with his family and friends. He never visits anyone, nor is he visited. He is perfectly insulated against sorrow . . . but he is not happy. He has no one to share special moments with, no one with whom he can feel emotion.

The Bible says that when we suffer, we are able to help others who suffer. There is a blessing to those who can identify with pain, especially if they have experienced their own pain. Paul called God the "Father of mercies and God of all comfort, who comforts us in all our tribulation, that we may be able to comfort those who are in any trouble, with the comfort with which we ourselves are comforted by God" (2 Corinthians 1:3-4). In the midst of trouble, God offers a whole new inventory of tools to help those around you. How blessed to talk with somebody who has been through exactly what we're experiencing! Happy are those who can sympathize with the sorrowing people around them.

Happiness Is Discovered When We Sorrow for Our Own Sin

In 2 Corinthians 7:10, we read, "For godly sorrow produces repentance leading to salvation, not to be regretted; but the sorrow of the world produces death." When was the last time you shed tears over the sin in your life? Generally in our culture, we simply don't deal with sin. The famed psychologist Carl Menninger, who studied the effects of sin in his famous book *Whatever Happened to Sin?*, noted that when an individual fails to deal with the wrongs in his life, he never takes a step toward getting better. We call ourselves victims, always blaming someone else for our faults. A thief doesn't own up to his sin; he blames it on his deprived childhood. A murderer doesn't admit his sin; he blames it on abuse. But when a man faces up to the things in his life that he knows violate the holiness of God, he mourns over his own sin.

Have you ever come to God so broken-hearted over your failure that you wept? The Bible says that doing so is a cleansing step toward holiness and happiness in life. Blessed are they who mourn, for they shall be comforted. The man who cannot mourn over his own sin can never know the comfort and forgiveness of God. The Lord doesn't forgive sin we won't confess. But when we come to God, acknowledging what we have done and weeping in realization that it was our sin which helped nail Christ to the cross, God begins the healing process in our lives. Our hurt leads to the blessing of God's comfort.

As you study the life of Paul, you'll find that the older he got, the less impressed he became with himself. In his first letter, Galatians, he wrote, "Paul, an apostle . . . " (Galatians 1:1). Seven years later, when he wrote his first letter to the Corinthians, he noted, "I am the least of the apostles, who am not worthy to be called an apostle" (1 Corinthians 15:9). Eight years after that, Paul said of himself, "To me, who am less than the least of all the saints . . . " (Ephesians 3:8). At this point Paul isn't talking about himself as an apostle, but as the least of all the saints. Late in his life, Paul wrote to his friend Timothy and said, "Christ Jesus came into the world to save sinners, of whom I am chief" (1 Timothy 1:15). In the span of a few years Paul went from being an apostle to being the chief sinner. The closer he got to the Lord, the more he realized the poverty of his own soul. Blessed are those who mourn over their own sin, shedding tears over the evil in their lives, for they can experience a wonderful peace in knowing that God cares and forgives them. They shall be comforted.

Happiness Is Discovered When We Suffer the Losses and the Crosses of Life

Sorrow has a value all its own. An old Arabian proverb says that "all sunshine makes a desert." You see, sorrow is the source for some of the greatest discoveries. The meaning of friendship and the meaning of love are often best found due to sorrow. It is in sorrow that a man discovers whether his faith is superficial or solid. In sorrow a man discovers God. The saddest thing in the world, according to James Reid, is not a soul that sorrows, but a heart so selfish and dull that nothing touches it. To sorrow is to love. "Mourning," according to Reid, "is indeed but another and deeper side of loving." The poet Robert Hamilton wrote, "I walked a mile with pleasure, and she chatted all the way; but left me none the wiser for all she had to say. I walked a mile with sorrow, and ne'er a word said she; but O! the things I learned from her, when sorrow walked with me."

How do you deal with sorrow? Perhaps you've lost a loved one, or gone through a divorce, or lost your job. How does a Christian deal with grief? I've heard preachers give out some pretty bad counsel over the years. We've warned people to rest on the sovereignty of God; that what has happened is God's will, and that injustices will be made right in the next world. We are guilty of substituting fatalism for faith, because many of life's disorders do not come from God. Some come from folly or sin. If I violate the principles of good health, God should not be blamed for my sickness and death. I've heard good people tell those in grief to resign themselves to sorrow, for that is the common lot of man. But the way the world deals with grief is far different from the way God tells us to deal with it.

First, God says to express grief, not repress it. Our culture says to bury the feelings. We don't want to be reminded of anything negative. But Jesus openly wept on at least three occasions. Expressing feeling is an emotional release, offering cleansing and freeing us to begin the journey toward hope.

Second, God says to face your loss, not replace it. Society's instruction is to get busy and fill your life with something else. Don't hang around a sad place. But that doesn't make it go away, it only buries the hurt like an emotional toxic waste. The pattern in the Bible is to allow the full effect of sorrow to settle into our souls. There are no shortcuts to recovery. A person who reviews his loss, thinks it through, talks about it to friends and his Lord, will begin to get through it.

Third, God says to reach out to others, not retreat from them. Our culture encourages us to leave grieving people alone, to "give them space." God's approach is the exact opposite. We are to grieve in community with one another. After Jesus' death, the disciples were all together, sharing their grief with one another. "Rejoice with those who rejoice," Paul tells us, "and weep with those who weep."

Fourth, God says to depend on the Comforter, not on the calendar. The normal counsel to one who is grieving is that "time heals all wounds." But the Bible says the Holy Spirit is the healer. The word Christ used to tell us that those who mourn shall be comforted is the very same word He used to explain the Holy Spirit. You may heal over time, but it is the Spirit doing the healing. The word is also translated "encouragement" or "made strong," because that's what the Spirit does when we mourn. In sadness, God is up to something. He wants to move you toward joy.

APPLICATION

1. How would you define *mourning*?

How does our culture view mourning?

Why do you think we are so uncomfortable with mourning and sorrow?

2. Does the Bible ask us to ignore sorrow?

What are some examples of mourning shown in Scripture?

3. How can sacrificing the present for the future bring sorrow?

How can it lead to joy?

Have you ever had to sacrifice something now for a greater joy later?

Why is that so difficult to do?

4. How did the Lord Jesus reveal Himself to be a man of compassion?

How can sympathizing with those who are suffering bring happiness?

What principles does Paul suggest in 2 Corinthians 1:3-4?

Have you ever had anyone suffer with you during a crisis? How did it help?

5. Read Psalm 51. How does David's sorrow over his sin lead to eventual joy?

What does Paul say happens through our sorrow in 2 Corinthians 7:10?

Why is sorrow over sin a necessary part of God's process of forgiveness?

The mourning Jesus showed is one of the characteristics that help us understand His humanity. Occasionally heretics will rise up claiming Jesus wasn't really a man but a spirit. But that argument has been destroyed on several occasions throughout history by looking at the fact that Jesus ate, got tired, got hungry and thirsty, bled, wept, and showed human compassion to those in pain. Jesus was fully man and fully God.

HAPPY ARE THE HARNESSED

Matthew 5:5

This chapter explores Christ's teaching about the meek and how meekness is actually a strength.

OUTLINE

While our culture seems to value overt displays of strength, Christ encourages us to manifest our meekness. Strength is not found in defeating others, but in harnessing one's power.

I. The Meaning of Meekness in the Old Testament
II. The Meaning of Meekness in the New Testament

A ccording to Jesus, everything we've been taught about getting ahead in this world is wrong. The world says, "Believe in yourself." Jesus says, "Believe in me." The world says, "Strive to be number one." Jesus says, "The last shall be first, and the first shall be last." The world says, "Winning isn't everything; it's the only thing." Jesus says, "He who finds his life will lose it, and he who loses his life for My sake will find it." The world says, "Don't get mad; get even." Jesus says, "Love your enemies." The world says, "Assert yourself." Jesus says, "Deny yourself." The world teaches us how to get ahead. Jesus teaches us how to give ourselves away. The world claims that the one with the most toys wins. Jesus says that you can gain the whole world, but if you lose your soul, you have nothing.

We are never more at odds with the world than when we try to understand the Beatitudes. Jesus keeps offering us paradoxes, claiming those who mourn will be happy, and the humble will be exalted. But when he comes to meekness, we recoil. Most of us aren't all that interested in meekness. It seems weak and soft. As Don McCullough has said, "Coaches don't rally teams with meekness, executives don't send sales people into the field with it, and politicians don't promise to lead by it." We're turned off by the thought of becoming a milktoast in a world that demands toughness.

There are Christians who seem to accept that understanding of meekness. They picture a passive, dependent personality—the Christian as a doormat. Perhaps they think it is somehow holy to be inferior. One modern critic of the Bible even said, "Live by it if you want, and it will come true for you. If you are meek in life, you will inherit the earth—six feet of it."

The Meaning of Meekness in the Old Testament

The great historian William Barclay noted that to modern ears, *meekness* seems to denote a weak, flabby, spineless creature, "lacking all virility, submissive and subservient to a fault, unable to stand up for himself or for anyone else." But that is far from the true meaning of the word. Jesus' statement "Blessed are the meek" comes from Psalm 37, which offers a context for understanding the concept of meekness.

"But those who wait on the LORD, they shall inherit the earth . . . But the meek shall inherit the earth . . . For those blessed by Him shall inherit the earth . . . Wait on the LORD, and keep His way, and he shall exalt you to inherit the land" (Psalm 37:9, 11, 22, 34). Twice the psalmist connects the idea of waiting with the inheritance of the land. That helps us get close to the true meaning of meekness in the Bible. In Hebrew thought, the man who is meek is the one who obediently accepts God's guidance and is therefore dear to the Lord. His life is strengthened and beautified by the gifts God gives him. Barclay said that meekness in the Old Testament is the "intentional reliance upon God to accomplish His will and His work in His way."

Meekness is not weakness; it is dependence upon God. To "inherit the earth" means to be successful, so the Bible says that those who are meek will find success. Those who come to the place where they are reliant on God and committed to His way no matter what will discover true success. This attitude toward life is the only way to be happy, the only method for living above the difficulties and despairs of life. That's why David began the first few verses of Psalm 37 with the words "trust in the LORD," "delight in the LORD," "commit your way to the LORD," and "rest in the LORD." If you do those things, you won't worry. You'll trust in God's guidance. You'll be delighted in His way. Meekness is coming to the place where you are willing to give everything up to God and say, "This isn't my problem, Lord. I'm relying on you." Like putty in God's hands, you will allow yourself to be molded and shaped by Him. As you yield to His purpose, you will find success in life. Meekness is submission to the will of God, trusting in Him fully, even when life doesn't seem to make sense.

Job illustrates this sort of attitude toward God. In one day Job lost everything he had, but he meekly accepted it. "The LORD gave, and the LORD has taken away; blessed be the name of the LORD," Job says in Job 1:21. He had lost his family, his farm, and all his wealth. But he stood before God in the midst of that disaster and said, "It's all in God's hands. Blessed be His name." In Job 13:15 he even says, "Though He slay me, yet will I trust Him." That's meekness: standing in the midst of disaster and knowing that God hasn't forgotten you or made a mistake. Paul was like that. A proud, arrogant Pharisee, when confronted by the Lord he meekly said, "Lord, what do you want me to do?" Mary was also like that. Imagine this young, unmarried girl confronted with the fact that she was pregnant even though she had not been with a man. Instead of worrying about the social cost, she said, "Behold the maidservant of the Lord! Let it be to me according to your word" (Luke 1:38). It's as though Mary were saying, "I'm in your hands, God. Do whatever you want with me."

When the Lord Jesus was in the Garden of Gethsemane, the weight of the world's sin coming down upon Him, He realized the pain He would have to endure by going to the Cross. In His humanity, Jesus struggled with the price He would have to pay. But as He prayed, He said, "Not as I will, but as you will." That's meekness. You may be in a difficult situation where you say, "Lord, I've done everything I know how to do to make things work, and it isn't working." You're fretting and upset. That's the time the meek person says, "God, I don't know what to do. I'm giving it up to you. I'm trusting in you." That's the meekness that Christ says will bring success.

The Meaning of Meekness in the New Testament

Meekness came to mean something else in Christ's day. Rather than referring to the control of God, it came to be seen as the control of oneself. The two are not diametrically opposed, for the person who is controlled by God will be in control of himself, filled with the Spirit and exercising self-control. The literal rendering of the word *meekness* in the New Testament is "power under control."

Paul lists meekness as one of the fruits of the Spirit, so when one is like Jesus Christ he will be meek. Jesus even referred to Himself as meek in Matthew 11:28-29. He had all power, but He kept it under control. Having power and insisting on using it all the time to maintain control is weakness. Having power and keeping it under control is meekness. The meek man doesn't get angry at people who are in the right, nor does he fail to get angry at those in the wrong. His power is under control. He acts gently even though he has the power to act with stern severity. Never is a man so strong as when he knows he has the potential to exert power, yet chooses not to do so. He walks in measured steps, the Holy Spirit acting as a governor on his life. He is meek, the opposite of weak.

I have sometimes heard Jesus described as weak, which is amazing when you consider His fearlessness and power. He got angry with the Pharisees for objecting to His healing a withered hand on the Sabbath. He let everyone know how He felt about child abusers, telling them they ought to have great rocks tied around their necks and be thrown into the sea. He strongly rebuked Peter for getting in the way of God's plan. Jesus wasn't weak. He took a firm stand for the right.

In the temple courts of His day, the priests set up a form of extortion. In those days, a Jew couldn't come to worship without a sacrifice, and the sacrifice had to be blessed by a priest. So the priests simply refused to bless any animals the people brought in themselves, insisting they buy sacrificial animals from the priests' own market. They began charging exorbitant prices, lining their own pockets with the extorted money of the people. So one day Jesus walked into their market with a whip and cleaned the place out. I can just see the money falling onto the floor, the birds and animals running loose, and the priests scrambling to get out of the way. Christ wasn't weak—He simply kept His power under control. He never seemed to get mad at those who hurt Him, but only at the injustices suffered by others. He is described in Scripture as a sheep headed toward slaughter, never getting angry at the insults and injuries He received. When they placed a crown of thorns on His head, He didn't cry out at the injustice. He accepted the things that came His way, even though they weren't fair, but lashed out in righteous anger at those things which hurt others. His anger was under control, displayed at the right time, in the right spirit, for the right reasons.

I think one of the things wrong with our modern culture is that we've lost the concept of righteous anger. We don't get mad at children being aborted or our society heading down the sewer. Jesus had a passion for those being led away from the truth. Meekness is not weakness. Weakness yields to one's nature, while meekness takes control over one's nature. "He who is slow to anger is better than the mighty, and he who rules his spirit than he who takes a city," Solomon said in Proverbs 16:32. A person in control of himself has deep strength in his spirit. He gets angry at the right things, but suffers many injustices. Much of life is made up of hard things and a meek person can survive them without complaint. Thomas Brown once said that meekness is "taking injuries like we take pills—not chewing them, but swallowing them whole." Life isn't always fair, and sometimes we'll be mistreated, but the meek person swallows the injustice. He has power under control and will experience the success of God because of it.

APPLICATION

1. How would you define *power*?

Why is power so valued in our culture?

How have you seen people wield power over others?

2. What is your first reaction to Christ's call to meekness?

How do you define *meekness*?

Why does Christ consider it important to the Christian life?

3. What does Psalm 37:1-6 tell us to do?

How does that demonstrate meekness?

What promises are we given in that passage?

4. What further commands are we given in verses 7-11?

What will the result of our actions be?

5. What do verses 16-26 recommend we do in the face of evil?

What principles for living the Christian life can you find in verses 27-40?

What promise does the Lord offer us in that passage as a hope to hold on to?

6. Is meekness weakness? Why or why not?

How can a meek person remain strong?

What would you have to do to put your power under control?

The Beatitudes are a form of Hebrew poetry, characterized by a literary device known as parallelism. One phrase is balanced against another phrase. You'll note that each of the Beatitudes offers an original phrase which includes a character quality: "Blessed are the meek," or "Blessed are the merciful . . ." That phrase is then paralleled by a promise such as, "For they shall inherit the earth." This balancing of thought reflects a careful crafting of words. Jesus knew what He wanted to say and probably said these same words more than once.

HAPPY ARE THE HUNGRY

Matthew 5:6

This chapter explores the happiness experienced by those who hunger after God.

OUTLINE

Developing a deep yearning for God is a sure route to happiness. Spiritual hunger, the desire for God in your inner being, can be filled through a relationship with Jesus Christ.

  I. Spiritual Hunger Is the Reality of Our Faith
 II. Spiritual Hunger Is the Requirement for our Growth
III. Lack of Spiritual Hunger Is the Reason for Our Failure

Blessed are those who hunger and thirst for righteousness, for they shall be filled" (Matthew 5:6). Hunger is something you come across every day. There are young businessmen whom we describe as "hungry" because they want to make the sale so badly that they'll do nearly anything. There are athletes whom we describe as "hungry" because they go all out to win. And there are people who so want to know God better that they can be described as "spiritually hungry." A.W. Tozer once noted that the great people of Christendom have had an insatiable hunger for God. The great missionary Hudson Taylor wrote, "I saw Him, and I sought Him, and I had Him, and I wanted Him." He was hungry for God. That's a characteristic of those who walk with God and experience the joy of knowing Him.

In Psalm 27:4, David describes his relationship with God by saying, "One thing have I desired of the LORD, that will I seek: That I may dwell in the house of the LORD all the days of my life, to behold the beauty of the LORD, and to inquire in His temple." The desire to know God was at the center of David's life. The sons of Korah reveal a similar theme in Psalm 42:1: "As the deer pants for the water brooks, so pants my soul for You, O God." And Psalm 63:1-2 reads, "O God, You are my God; early will I seek You; my soul thirsts for You; my flesh longs for You in a dry and thirsty land where there is no water. So I have looked for You in the sanctuary, to see Your power and Your glory."

The psalmists had a deep hunger for God. Throughout Psalm 119 you can find illustrations of that desire. In verse 34 the author says he wants God's word in his heart. Verse 40 speaks of longing after God's truth, and verse 58 entreats God's favor with his whole heart. "I cry out with my whole heart," we read in verse 145. All of those verses reveal a longing to know God. If you've ever worked with someone who approached the job in a half-hearted way, you know how frustrating it can be. But the psalmist was whole-hearted when it came to knowing God. To give everything toward seeking Him—that is the essence of spiritual hunger. All of the great men and women of God have had it. Moses, Elijah, Isaiah, David, and John had a hunger for God. Luther, St. Francis, Pliny, and Thomas á Kempis thirsted after the Lord. They sought the Lord and weren't satisfied by anything other than a close walk with Him.

You know, I am convinced that we have as much of God as we really want. You may claim to want more of God in your life, but you already have as much as you want. If you've ever been thirsty on a hot day, you know what it is to long for water. Most of us don't long for God with that sort of passion. We want a convenient religion—one that can fit into our schedules without too much difficulty. We want God in our lives, but we don't want to be fanatics. Yet Jesus said that it is the spiritually hungry and thirsty who will be happy, for they'll be filled with the satisfying presence of the Lord.

Spiritual Hunger Is the Reality of Our Faith

This verse may be the most demanding of the Beatitudes. Jesus wants His people to hunger and thirst after God. Yet it also shows how Jesus views our struggles. He did not say, "Blessed are they who attain righteousness," or none of us could be blessed. Christ didn't permit happiness only to the spiritually mature but to all who desire and seek after maturity. If you have a desire within you to know God better, to understand His Word better, and to live this life more authentically for the Lord, the very wanting of it is evidence that you already belong to God. In our world today, many people call themselves Christians, but they don't seek after the things of God. They don't have any desire for the things of God. They have an entry-level relationship with the Almighty, so they assume they are on their way to heaven and need nothing more. But if there isn't a holy dissatisfaction in your heart about your spiritual life, and a hungering and thirsting to go further with God, then there is something missing in your faith. I love God, but the Bible tells me that I am to grow in my ability to love God. I love God's Word, but the Bible says that I am to be growing in my hunger for it. Spiritual hunger is a blessed evidence within our hearts that we truly belong to Him. If you are unhappy with your spiritual life, that's a good sign. So am I. I want to know God better. That's simply the reality of being a Christian.

Spiritual Hunger Is the Requirement for Our Growth

A rich young ruler once came to Jesus in search of eternal life. Jesus was impressed with the man, for he was attractive, successful, and seeking the right things. The Bible tells us that Jesus loved him. So the Lord told him to sell everything he had and give the money away. I don't believe that simply having money was the problem. The issue was one of spiritual hunger. In essence, Jesus was saying, "If you don't want me more than you want money, you're not going to make it." Christ wants us to have a hunger for Himself.

Early in His ministry, Jesus was being followed by great crowds of people. They wanted the miracles and the ministry of Jesus but not the commitment He demanded. One day the Lord simply stood up and said, "Let me tell you what it's going to take if you want to follow me. You will have to deny yourself. You will have to leave home and family. There will be divisions in relationships. You may be called by God to suffer hurts, injustice, and pain. But unless you do those things and make me first, you are not worthy to be my disciples." Suddenly there were no longer any crowds following Jesus. The thing that separates people from the Lord is the thing we call spiritual hunger—the desire to know God above all else. If you want to grow in Christ, you must have spiritual hunger.

The Lack of Spiritual Hunger Is the Reason for Our Spiritual Failure

Sometimes we don't want to be Christians. We claim that we do, but we aren't willing to do the hard things necessary. I've seen businessmen and athletes achieve success by sheer force of their desires, but I know few Christians willing to sacrifice anything to find God. Dan Henning, a former head coach in the National Football League, once told me that what separates a great quarterback from a good quarterback is the intangibles. The great ones have an inner toughness and desire to succeed. They hunger to win football games.

One of the secrets to success and achievement is desire. To be a mighty man or woman of God requires first a great desire in your heart to know God. If you're happy just to be in the game, you won't accomplish much for Him. The secret to making a difference for God in this world is desire. The Apostle Paul was a man of desire. He had some great experiences, including three visions of Jesus which included things he couldn't even describe. At the end of his life, Paul said that the desire of his life was to know Christ. He hadn't yet arrived but was pressing ahead toward God. The closer he got to his goal, the more he gave himself to it. It's easy to be a mediocre Christian, with nice friends, celebratory worship, and interesting classes about the faith. But if we allow the perks of the church to run our lives, we will always remain on one immature level with God. And the truth is, we'll never really be happy. There is no challenge, no excitement, and no adventure in mediocrity. If you really want to know God, if you really want to be happy, you'll develop a hunger and thirst for Him.

So consider two insightful questions for your spiritual life. First, are you satisfied with yourself? The Puritans used to say, "He has the most need of righteousness who least wants it." If you are smug and self-satisfied, you aren't hungry, and God wants you hungry. A person hungering and thirsting after righteousness has a desire for God's Word. It's funny how that spiritual hunger works, for it's the exact opposite of physical hunger. With physical hunger, you get hungry when you don't eat. Once you've eaten, you are no longer hungry. With spiritual hunger, the more you eat, the hungrier you get. When you stop partaking of spiritual food though the Word of God, you lose your appetite. The more you get into the Bible, the more you begin to make sense of God's Word in your life and the greater your appetite. I've got friends who are memorizing the book of Romans, and their spiritual appetite has increased dramatically since they began.

Perhaps there was a time in your life when you were really hungry for God's Word. If you're not now, it's time you began reading your Bible again. As you begin to partake of the Word, your appetite for it will return. If you've gone through the process of pushing God out of your life, force-feed yourself. Sit down, open up your Bible, and start to read. If you start to fall asleep, read it aloud. Keep reading, and eventually God will speak to your heart. There will be a new fire in your soul. You'll experience a new love for God. The more you do it, the more you'll want to do it. If you are struggling with the language, get yourself a modern translation of the Scriptures. If you don't spend time reading your Bible, you'll never develop a hunger and thirst for God. And without a hunger and thirst for righteousness, you cannot be filled. Your life will be one of unfulfillment, never filled up with the Lord.

There is a second question that you need to consider, one that you must answer in the quietness of your own heart. As you examine your relationship with the Lord, are you hungry for God? You have as much of Him as you really want. Are you satisfied with where you are with God? Or do you want more? Those who hunger and thirst after righteousness will one day be filled. If you want to have that satisfaction of being filled up with God, develop your hunger for Him now.

APPLICATION

1. What does it mean to hunger after God?

Have you ever known anyone who hungered after the Lord? How would you describe his or her life?

In what ways have you hungered after God?

2. How does David describe hungering after God in Psalm 27?

How do the sons of Korah describe their hungering after the Lord in Psalm 42?

What does it mean to thirst for God, according to Psalm 63?

Can you relate to those psalms? When have you ever felt that you needed God that much?

3. Do you agree or disagree with the statement, "We all have as much of God as we want"? Why?

Is it a good sign to be unsatisfied with your spiritual life? Why?

4. How is spiritual hunger a requirement for spiritual growth?

How did David, Moses, Elijah, Daniel, and Job all demonstrate their spiritual hunger?

Did the crowds following Jesus have the same hunger as the twelve disciples? Explain your answer.

5. For what do you hunger?

Are you satisfied with your spiritual life?

What would you like to see change in your life?

6. Take a moment right now to write a psalm to the Lord describing how you feel and where you would like to be in your relationship with Him.

HAPPY ARE THE HELPERS

Matthew 5:7

This chapter will explore the practice of mercy and what the result of merciful behavior will be.

OUTLINE

In a merciless world, Christ has called His people to manifest mercy.

   I. **What Is Mercy?**
  II. **How Is Mercy Expressed?**
 III. **What Are the Results of Mercy?**

B lessed are the merciful, for they shall obtain mercy"
(Matthew 5:7). Some years ago Lorraine Hansberry wrote a
successful play entitled *A Raisin in the Sun*. In the play, an
African-American family inherits ten thousand dollars from a life
insurance policy, and the mother sees that money as a chance to
help her family escape from the ghetto and move into a real house
in the country. Her daughter, a brilliant student, wants to use the
money to fulfill her dream of going to medical school. But her son
convinces everyone that he can take the money, start a business
with a friend, and accomplish all those things. He promises the
family that if they will give him the money, he'll return all the
blessings their hard lives have denied them.

Against her better judgment, the mother gives her son the
money, believing that he deserves a chance to succeed. But the
son's "friend" skips town with the money, and the young man
must face his family and admit that all their hopes for the future
have been dashed. His sister lashes out at him with a barrage of
ugly epithets. She calls him every despicable thing you can imagine. Her contempt has no limits, and when her mother interrupts
by saying, "I thought I taught you to love your brother," the girl
replies, "Love him? There's nothing left to love!"

Then, in a way that shows she understands mercy, the mother
responds,

> There is always something left to love. If you ain't
> learned that, you ain't learned nothin'. Have you cried
> for that boy today? I don't mean for yourself and the
> family because we lost all that money. I mean for him, for
> what he's been through, and what it's done to him.
> Child, when do you think it's the time to love somebody
> the most? When they done good and made things easy
> for everybody? Well then, you ain't through learnin'
> because that ain't the time at all. It's when he's at his
> lowest and can't believe in himself 'cause the world
> done whipped him so. When you starts measurin' some-
> body, measure him right, child. Measure him right.
> Make sure you done taken into account what hills and
> valleys he come through before he got to wherever he is.

That's mercy. And child, you need to learn mercy.

What Is Mercy?

Mercy is love that is given when it is not deserved. It is forgiveness that is given when it is not earned. It is a gift that flows like a refreshing stream to quench the fires of angry, condemning words. It is called mercy, and in our day it's almost a forgotten quality.

Some time ago, *Christianity Today* reported that seminary students were upset about something a reporter had learned. It seems a couple of researchers decided to find out if those preparing for the ministry were also good samaritans. They met individually with forty seminary students and taped interviews with them as they walked along a particular path. They were asked questions about their careers and concerns for the future; then they were asked to talk about the parable of the Good Samaritan. On cue, a hired actor dressed as a bum would groan and slump to the ground in front of them. More than half the students walked right on by. Some literally stepped over the slumped body as they hurried to tell their story.

Those seminarians are probably no different from most of us. We live in a world with a closed heart, closed hand, and closed home. Many of us have shut ourselves up because of the risk of involvement. The hard, isolated, and uncompassionate characteristic of society has crept into our lives, so that we don't want to worry about anybody else. "Think about Number One," the world says to us. "Don't open your eyes to the needs of people. Look after yourself first."

But the Bible suggests a different standard. The Greek word for "mercy" literally means "full of pity." It describes someone with a sympathetic heart and is often used to describe the Lord Jesus. In Matthew chapter fifteen we read of the compassion Christ had for a demon-possessed woman. In chapter eighteen Jesus shows compassion for a man in debt and in chapter twenty, He has compassion on two blind men. And in Mark five we read about Christ's compassion for a man in need of deliverance. For Christians, mercy is a Spirit-guided ability to manifest practical, compassionate, and cheerful love toward someone who is suffering. In the New Testament it most often refers to those who might be easily ignored—the crippled, the sick, the deformed, the aged, or the mentally ill. Those less fortunate than ourselves are the ones to whom we ought to show mercy. Mercy is one of the noblest virtues. It dares to express tenderness in the midst of a harsh and cruel world. Our world preaches that you'll be happiest when you forget about others and focus on yourself, but Jesus said that those who exhibit mercy will be happy.

How Is Mercy Expressed?

In Luke chapter ten, Jesus told a story of a Samaritan who was willing to step out of the context of his day and act differently than the lawyers and priests of the first century. The Lord said that a man fell among thieves, was beaten, bruised, and left for dead. It's clear that religion wasn't the solution he needed, for all the religious people passed by: a priest, a Levite, and a lawyer who spent his time studying the Law of God. But a Samaritan, who was hated by the Jews, became the hero of Jesus' story. He stopped to minister to this unfortunate one, to a man he didn't know. Luke 10 says that he had compassion on him. The Samaritan's heart was moved by what he saw. He took that bleeding man and bound up his wounds, used an antiseptic, and poured oil on him to soothe the pain. Rather than just saying a prayer for him, the Samaritan exhibited real love by taking care of someone else in need.

A careful reading of the story reveals that it cost the Samaritan to minister. The act of mercy on his part wasn't without cost. There was no "easy grace." He took out of that which was his own to help another. He paid for the oil and the medicine. He gave the wounded man transportation. He gave up time in his schedule to care for this stranger, and even paid for the man to stay at an inn until he was better. You can't show mercy without having it cost you something. And all this was done by a despised Samaritan, who wouldn't even have been greeted by a passing Jew. Christ noted that to put pressure on the religious people of His day. In essence, Jesus was saying, "Even the hated Samaritan knows how to show mercy. Why don't you?"

At the end of the story, Jesus asked, "Which of these three do you think was neighbor to him who fell among the thieves—the priest, the Levite, or the good Samaritan?" Then, without waiting for a reply, the Lord said, "He who showed mercy on him." Mercy is the quality of the Good Samaritan, and Jesus instructs us to "go and do likewise." Mercy is what the Samaritan did when he reached out to someone who could not pay him back, who was hurting and in need. We need to learn to express that virtue in the church. It's easy to want to travel in circles where everything is beautiful and everyone is like us. But the Bible says that we'll find happiness when we learn to show mercy to those who aren't quite as nicely dressed or as educated and refined as ourselves.

I read an article recently about a young Christian nurse who decided she was going to manifest mercy. One of her patients was a woman in a vegetative state. She'd had a cerebral aneurism and was completely brain dead, unaware of anything around her. To make it easier to care for her, the staff became emotionally detached. The patient was treated like a "thing," not a person, by the hospital staff. But this young nurse couldn't treat anyone like that. She talked to the patient, offering friendliness and encouragement, even though she knew the patient couldn't hear or respond. When the nurse was scheduled to work on a holiday, she made it a point to be extra positive. As she was taking care of things in the room, she suddenly noticed the patient was looking at her, crying. It was the only emotion she had ever shown, and it changed the attitude of the entire staff toward her. The nurse later said that she owed that patient quite a lot. Without that experience, she might never have known what it was like to give herself completely to someone who could offer nothing in return. That's the true spirit of mercy.

What Are the Results of Mercy?

Jesus said that the merciful would obtain mercy. If you show mercy to someone else, you get mercy back. We have received mercy from God, so we ourselves can show mercy to others. As we understand the depth of God's mercy, we are compelled to be merciful toward others.

Jesus once said, "For with what judgment you judge, you will be judged; and with the measure you use, it will be measured back to you" (Matthew 7:2). If you forgive others, God will also forgive you. But if you are unforgiving, you will find the Lord that same way. "For judgment is without mercy to the one who has shown no mercy," it says in James 2:13. As a man judges, so will he be judged. If mercy is the characteristic of God, then someone who practices it will become more and more like God every day. But he who makes no attempt to show mercy distances himself from God and demonstrates that he does not know Him.

Peter once asked Jesus how many times he should forgive someone. Thinking himself generous, Peter suggested the number seventy. But the Lord laughed off that number and suggested it was more like seventy times seven. Then Jesus told the story of a man who owed a king a great sum of money but was unable to pay it back. He was mercifully forgiven the debt, but that same man then went out and had another man arrested for not paying him back ten dollars! The king was furious when he found out about it and had the ungrateful wretch arrested until he could pay back every penny. And the Lord finished his story by saying, "So my heavenly Father also will do to you if each of you, from his heart, does not forgive his brother his trespasses" (Matthew 18:35). What made it mandatory that the ten dollar debt be forgiven? The fact that his own huge debt had been cancelled.

We have been forgiven a great debt by our Heavenly Father, one we could never repay. Our sin debt was so great that no amount of good works or sacrifice could ever take care of it. "The wages of sin is death," we are told in Romans 6:23. But when Christ died on the cross, He forgave us freely of everything we have ever done. He has shown us great mercy. So what should we do when confronted by someone who needs our mercy? We are to extend mercy. It's our responsibility, by the grace of God, to show mercy to those around us. It doesn't always happen in the church because we want people to live up to our expectations and "earn" our love, but that's not the system Christ put into place. He wants us to love others, even when they don't deserve it. We are all flawed human beings in need of mercy.

In Morton Thompson's novel, *Not as a Stranger*, a young doctor accuses an older physician of malpractice. Brilliant and capable, but impatient and intolerant, the young doctor sits before a review committee to discuss the charges. The men on the committee are older and ask the young man not to act hastily, but to consider the actions of the older doctor as a difference of opinion. Any man in the zealousness of youth tends to judge others more harshly. But that young doctor will not retract his accusation. So the president of the medical association leans across his desk, looks the young man right in the eyes, and says, "If you persist in bringing formal charges, then be sure of one thing: don't ever, ever, as long as you live, make a mistake." The way we treat others is the way we'll be treated. And the good news is that if you will show mercy to others, even when they don't deserve it, the result will be happiness.

Ask God to give you sensitivity to those around you. Look for people with needs, and then reach out in mercy and meet them. The world says to look out for yourself, but the Lord says to look out for others. The world wants you to believe that you'll be happy when you take care of yourself, but nobody is really happy in a selfish world—they're alone. Happiness is found in ministering to others. The merciful will obtain mercy and will find true happiness in being merciful to others.

APPLICATION

1. What is mercy?

Can you think of some examples of Jesus showing mercy to others?

Why will mercy lead to happiness?

2. In Matthew 18:23-35, who shows mercy?

Who fails to show mercy, and what effect does it have on him?

What warning does Jesus offer us at the very end of that parable?

3. How does mercy affect us? In other words, what do we receive when we show mercy to someone?

What does Matthew 7:2 have to say about that?

What does James 2:13 add?

4. What is the source for a Christian's mercy?

To whom should we show mercy?

What should we do if the other person has not been merciful to us?

5. How does our culture speak against mercy?

Rather than mercy, what does the world value?

How can a Christian use mercy to make an impact on the world?

6. Have you ever known anyone who offered mercy when none was expected?

What difference did it make to the people involved?

How is God calling you to manifest mercy?

DID YOU KNOW?

Jesus criticized the Pharisees for a complete lack of mercy. They would tithe, but they wouldn't show mercy. Without mercy, their religion became a selfish act.

HAPPY ARE THE HOLY

Matthew 5:8

In this chapter, we will look at the effects of a holy life.

OUTLINE

Jesus talks about happiness in terms most people won't accept. You won't often hear someone say in a lecture, "If you really want to be happy, have a pure heart." But Jesus said that very thing, and if we understand what a pure heart is, we'll know that only the pure know true happiness.

I. **What Does It Mean to Be Pure in Heart?**
II. **What Does It Mean When It Says "Heart"?**
III. **What Does It Mean When It Says the Impure of Heart Cannot See God?**

B lessed are the pure in heart, for they shall see God"
(Matthew 5:8). Those words in the Greek can literally be
translated, "Happy are the pure in heart, for they and they
alone will see God." The first time I realized the meaning of those
words, I was a little chagrined. Who is pure? What is the standard?

We've seen how the humble are happy, and how those who are
hurting can be happy, but now Jesus comes out and tells us that if
we truly want to be happy, we ought to be holy. That's hard to do.
I received a letter from a young man recently who told me he had
been traveling. Since he was away from his wife, he was thinking
about going out to see a pornographic movie, but he turned on
the radio instead and heard our program. He wrote to me,
explaining how unhappy he was with himself, and asking for help.
I think that young man represents tens of thousands of men who
are involved in ungodly activities and hating themselves for it.
Satan tempts us with the lure of pleasure, but those activities
always result in unhappiness. Unholy people aren't happy. Sin
doesn't ever produce the joy it promises. So Christ says, "If you
want to be happy, be holy."

What Does It Mean to Be Pure in Heart?

The dictionary says that *purity* is "freedom from foreign mix-
tures or matter; cleanness; freedom from foulness or dirt; freedom
from guilt or defilement." To be pure means that you are living a
"clean" life. If you'll look carefully at this passage of Scripture,
you'll find that Jesus was very concerned about the lifestyles of the
Pharisees. They were pure on the outside, but rotten on the inside.
Christ compared them to whitewashed tombs, which looked nice
outside but contained rotting corpses on the inside. The Lord
criticized them for putting on a display of piety so that they would
look good to others while retaining an evil heart. God wants us to
be holy throughout, having been cleansed from sin and changed
by the Spirit of God. Rather than simply maintaining an outward
obedience, the Lord wants us to have an inner holiness with an
attitude of love for God and others. We aren't merely to be clean
on the outside, but on the inside, in the heart.

What Does It Mean When It Says "Heart"?

The Greeks thought the heart was the center of thinking, so a modern reader could translate the word *mind* for heart. In other words, God wants us to have a clean mind, not just go through the motions of doing the right things. In Scripture, the "heart" is always seen as the inside part of a man, the seat of his personality and the center of his thinking process. Proverbs 23:7 reads, "As he thinks in his heart, so is he." To have a clean heart is to have a clean mind.

When Christ says, "Blessed are the pure in heart," He is encouraging us to have a clean mind before God, not corrupted with evil or impurities. "Keep your heart with all diligence," Solomon says in Proverbs 4:23, "for out of it spring the issues of life." In other words, if you get your heart right, you won't have to worry about the outside. Your actions will follow what your mind is thinking. Godliness doesn't move from the outside in but from the inside out. If you get your heart right, you'll live a holy life. And one of the benefits of a holy life is the happiness of seeing God.

One of my favorite Old Testament stories is the calling of David. When God called David's predecessor, Saul, to be the king, He chose a tall, handsome, powerful man. Saul looked great on the outside. But Saul had a problem with his heart. He just didn't want to follow God. He routinely violated God's standards, until God finally got fed up. Saul was finished. He was not going to be king anymore, nor would his ancestors sit on the throne of Israel. Instead, the Bible says that "the Lord sought out for Himself a man after His own heart." And God selected David.

David wasn't perfect—anyone who has read the man's life knows that. He made a number of mistakes, some of them big. But David had it where it counted: the heart. He was a man after God's own heart. To seek after the things of God, and to be willing to obey Him no matter what the cost, is to have a heart for God. That's the sort of person Jesus was describing in the Beatitudes.

What Does It Mean When It Says the Impure of Heart Cannot See God?

You may get discouraged as you read about being pure in heart. I've had people say to me, "Pastor, I don't have any hope. No matter how hard I try, I still have the defilement of the world in me. I just can't be pure!" But we have to keep in mind that there are different kinds of purity.

First, there is perfect purity, the kind we will one day have in heaven. That's the time we Christians "shall be like Him, for we shall see Him as He is" (1 John 3:2). On that day, every single person who has put his trust in God is going to be one hundred percent pure, just as Christ Himself is pure. We will be as holy as God. That's perfect purity, but it's out there in the future.

Second, there is positional purity, which is what Christ has done for us through His sacrifice. Remember, God says we have to be holy, but none of us can achieve holiness. If we could, Christ would never have had to come. We are all lost in sin, and it is impossible for any of us to be completely sinless and pure. But God saw mankind's plight, knew we were lost, and sent His Son to earth to show the world what it's like to live a perfect life. Jesus came and died on a cross as a sacrifice for all mankind, to pay the penalty for our sins. We can't be pure in our own strength, but if we understand what Christ has done for us and put our trust in Him, He will take away our sins and give us His righteousness. When you have received the righteousness of Jesus Christ, God no longer counts your sin against you. He looks at you and sees that you are positionally pure due to the gracious sacrifice of His Son.

I have put my trust in Christ, so when God looks at me, He sees that my heart is clean. Even though I'm a flawed human being who has failed time after time, God looks down and sees the righteousness of Christ. He accepts me because the righteousness of Christ has been credited to me—I am pure in Jesus. Remember, I'm not pure in David Jeremiah. I am righteous in the Son of God. When the Lord died on that cross, He paid the complete penalty for it, then imputed His righteousness to me. It's the greatest exchange that has ever taken place, for when God looks at me now, He sees my positional purity. That's why I will one day see God! In the purity of Jesus Christ, I have the guarantee that I will be with Him forever. Not because I'm good, but because His goodness has been granted to me.

Third, there is practical purity, the everyday living sort of purity. The Bible says as a Christian I am righteous, so now the Lord expects me to live like the righteous man I have become. Sanctification is being in practice what you already are in position. It is living each day in light of the righteousness of Christ. God wants me pure, but that purity is a challenge. Right now all Christians have positional purity, and some day each of us will have perfect purity, but we seem to have a lot of trouble putting our purity into practice.

To do so, you've got to have a strategy. Job 31:1 speaks of making a covenant with your eyes, so that as you begin putting purity into practice, you'll commit to watching only pure things. We used to sing a chorus with our children that went like this: "Oh be careful little eyes what you see; Oh be careful little eyes what you see; For the Father up above is looking down in love, so be careful little eyes what you see." The eyes are the window to the soul. They are the gate through which most impurity gets into your heart and mind. If there has ever been a time in which Christians needed a covenant with their eyes, it is in twentieth-century America. Everywhere you go there is visual stimuli to steer you away from God. You can't drive down a street or walk through an airport without billboards or television or advertisements flashing something impure. So make a covenant with your eyes regarding what you will gaze at and ponder. Be wary of the books you read, the movies you watch, and the magazines you look at. If you want to develop practical purity, make a covenant with your eyes.

Another thing you can do is to consecrate your mind. "As a man thinks in his heart, so is he," the Bible tells us. The heart, according to the Lord Jesus, is the seat of indwelling sin. Evil thoughts, adultery, murder, theft, covetousness, wickedness, and fornication all come from the heart of man. As far back as Noah's time, God perceived that "every intent of the thoughts of his heart was only evil continually" (Genesis 6:5). So we are to focus our minds on good things. "Whatever things are true, whatever things are noble, whatever things are just, whatever things are pure, whatever things are lovely, whatever things are of good report, if there is any virtue and if there is anything praiseworthy—meditate on these things. The things which you learned and received and heard and saw in me, these do, and the God of peace will be with you" (Philippians 4:8-9). Don't fall into the trap of believing you can't control what you think. You may not be able to totally control it, but you can certainly harness it and get it going in the right direction. You can decide not to expose yourself to evil things so that you won't be pondering them.

If you want to begin practicing purity, commit yourself to Bible memory. Find a powerful verse that speaks to some important area of your life, and then keep repeating it to yourself. Think through the verse, so that you can remember it without looking it up in your Bible. Memorization is important because you can't always determine when you'll need a thought from God, and you can't always run and get your Bible to find the proper passage that speaks to the need at hand. Hide God's Word in your heart, and it will keep you from sin. When your mind is filled with God's truth, it won't be filled with impurities. Ask the Lord to help you internalize truth, so that you can take it out and use it when necessary. "How can a young man cleanse his way?" the psalmist asks, then answers, "By taking heed according to Your word" (Psalm 119:9).

Christian, learn to counteract Satan's strategy in your life. Satan has a strategy for you, just like he does for me. He knows me inside out; he knows everything he can do to upset me or discourage me. He'll use the dumbest things to discourage me, but I've been working to counteract his plan. You see, having a plan is critical to developing practical purity. I once had a man come to me who was struggling with his thought life. He was all right during the day, but he really had a tough time going home. Then he told me that he worked downtown and walked home every day—right through the seedy part of town with adult bookstores and pornography places on either side. He said it was the shortest route home, but I encouraged him to find a longer way. I mean, this guy was struggling in his thought life but making the same mistake every day. Sometimes all it takes is a little counteraction!

If you're struggling with purity, analyze the enemy. Where does he attack? When? How do the attacks most often begin? Look for ways to fight back. God wants you to be holy, because He is holy. He desires you to be like Himself. Francois Muriac, a French Canadian writer, has talked openly about his struggles with fleshly temptation. He wanted to be pure but couldn't find a good reason to support his desire. Marriage didn't cure his lust, self-discipline didn't master it, and repression failed to make it go away. Then he read the words of Jesus in Matthew 5:8: "Blessed are the pure in heart, for they shall see God." In that, he found a reason to be pure. Impurity separates us from God, and Muriac wanted to be close to God. His desire for spiritual intimacy with God became so great in his heart that he would not allow physical impurity to get in the way. If you want to know Him, cultivate purity in your life.

1. What does it mean to be pure in heart?

Is it possible for us to be holy?

Does God see us as holy?

What is the difference between positional holiness and practical holiness?

2. Why is our holiness important to the Lord?

Why did Jesus criticize the Pharisees for their outward holiness?

What is our motivation for holiness?

3. What do the following passages reveal about our purity?

Psalm 15

Proverbs 4:23

Romans 6:11, 14

2 Corinthians 7:1

Hebrews 12:14

1 Peter 1:14-16

4. What do you suppose it means that David was "a man after God's own heart"?

What principles for holiness does Paul offer in 1 Corinthians 9:24-27?

What does Paul suggest to the Philippians in 4:8-9?

5. How can we begin to develop a holy life, according to Romans 12:1-2?

What does it mean to transform our minds? How do we do it?

Why is Scripture memory significant in transforming our minds?

Make a list of the top ten Bible verses you would like to memorize. Select passages which will help you do battle with temptation.

6. How does Satan try to involve you in sin?

What could you do differently to make it harder for Satan to win?

7. Take some time to pray about your holiness. Make sure to ask the Lord to forgive your sin, and then ask Him to make you strong in the spiritual battle.

HAPPY ARE THE HEALERS

Matthew 5 : 9

*This chapter will explore the role of peacemakers
in our world.*

OUTLINE

Man is constantly searching for peace but rarely finds it. Jesus offers us a glimpse at the true peacemakers of the world and the role they can play in our society.

  I. **Three Kinds of Peace**
    A. Peace with God
    B. Peace of God
    C. Peace from God
 II. **What Is a Peacemaker?**
III. **Where Are Peacemakers Found?**

B lessed are the peacemakers, for they shall be called sons of God" (Matthew 5:9). Humanity's quest for peace has been illustrated throughout the years by architecture. The Statue of Liberty offers a gesture of peace to those who come to our shores. The Statue of Shalom in Israel looks over the harbor at Haifa to remind people that there is another way. In front of Tokyo station is the statue of a man with his arms outstretched to heaven, while underneath is the Greek word *agape*—love. In almost every part of the world you can find some symbolic representation of man's quest for peace. Yet for all our labors, there is little peace in the world.

Three Kinds of Peace

The problem is not with nations but with the nature of man. As long as man remains separated from God and refuses to follow His divine plan for life, he will never be able to know any true peace. Man keeps trying, with peace treaties and ambassadors and the United Nations peace-keeping forces, but it all proves to be awfully frustrating. While peace is being talked about on one front, a war breaks out on another. "There is no peace to the wicked," says the prophet Isaiah, "for the wicked are like the troubled sea whose waves dredge up mire and dirt." As long as he determines in his heart to have none of God, he cannot have peace. He cannot have it individually, corporately, in his family, or in his country. He will not know peace until things are straightened out in his heart with God. We were created by God; only He has the plan, for He put all things together. God alone knows what brings peace, and He says that until we accept the Prince of Peace, there isn't any chance of getting out of the war zone. So we fight at home, at work, at church, and among nations—all because we don't have peace.

God's Word tells us about the nature of peace and describes at least three kinds of peace.

Peace with God

In Romans 5:1, Paul says, "Therefore, having been justified by faith, we have peace with God through our Lord Jesus Christ." God is not my enemy, though I've been at war with Him since I was born. My old depraved nature is at war with God. We are not born good and then go bad, as some think. Scripture is clear that man is born in sin. Children come into this world screaming for their own way, at war with God. But while we were at war with Him, He sent His only Son, Jesus Christ, into this world. He paid the penalty for all our sins when He died on the cross; so now the war is over. We can have peace with God through Jesus Christ.

When I explain the Gospel to people and they accept Christ into their lives, they often talk about having peace with God. Their war with God has been brought to an end. Without peace with God, we can never be peacemakers. We have no peace, so we cannot share it with anyone else. We can't give away what we don't have. In order to become peacemakers, we must have peace with God. That means coming to terms with what Christ has done on the Cross, taking away our sins and creating a relationship between us and God. When we became Christians, we were given peace with God.

Peace of God

Many Christians have peace with God but don't have the peace of God. That's why Christian bookstores are filled with so many self-help books. When I go into a bookstore, I see all these books about how we can straighten out our lives, and it makes me wonder what message they send to non-Christians. It would seem we really don't have our lives together. Why is it that so many Christians who have peace with God never get to the place of having the peace of God in their lives?

In John 14:27, the Lord Jesus said to His disciples, "Peace I leave with you, My peace I give to you; not as the world gives do I give to you. Let not your heart be troubled, neither let it be afraid." Christ wanted His people to have peace in their lives, no matter what they were facing. Without His peace, we're a troubled lot. He wants to give us the very peace of God. Do you have the inner calmness, the quiet assurance within you that all is well? Can you say with the Psalmist, "I will both lie down in peace, and sleep; for You alone, O LORD make me dwell in safety"? Can you remain peaceful in the face of chaotic circumstances? We all live in a war zone. Our neighborhoods face terrible troubles, there is great financial strain, and we struggle with job-related tensions. But if you have the peace of God, you can rest in peace.

Peace from God

There is a third kind of peace that we experience when facing a major decision. God doesn't have a magic instruction book, where you can turn to a particular page to discover His answer to your question. Instead, His book offers timeless principles that draw His people to Himself. As we begin to fill our minds with His principles, things become clear. He has already given us several clear "thou shalt not's" and some "thou shalt's," so where we sometimes get stumped is in the gray areas where we must judge between what is good and what is best. The choices may look equally acceptable, so we need the peace of God to guide us.

Colossians 3:15 reads, "Let the peace of God rule in your hearts," and that verse offers some great advice for deciding a course of action. After we have read our Bible and talked to Christian friends about our choices, we can ask the Lord to give us peace about our decision. It's okay to pray, "Lord, I don't know what to do in this situation, so I'm going to go this way. Please give me your peace." God can give us His peace in the major decisions of our lives after we've exhausted our ability to study the principles. Sometimes we just know in our hearts which choice is correct. When I was pastoring in Fort Wayne, Indiana, I was asked to pastor a church in California. Both churches were great situations, and I really didn't know what to do. I'd make up my mind one way, then change it the next day. Finally I told the Lord, "I think I'm supposed to go to California. Please give me a peace about my decision." And He did. I've never again doubted that it was the right decision, because I've experienced the peace of God.

What Is a Peacemaker?

Christ says that those with peace will be happy—blissful, joy-filled, ecstatic people. They know in their hearts that they are at peace with God. They have a certainty that they are no longer under condemnation but have been set free from sin. They are righteous in the eyes of God, and that allows them to become peacemakers. The man or woman who has peace can help other people find peace with God. In one sense, a peacemaker is an evangelist, because he goes about finding people at war with God and sharing the peace of Christ with them. Whenever I preach the Gospel and tell people how to know Jesus Christ, I have functioned as a peacemaker. If you are sharing your faith with others, you have become a peacemaker, and the Bible says there is great joy in being a peacemaker. For me, the greatest joy I've ever known has been introducing other people to the Lord Jesus. It's the most wonderful experience you can have. If you're not sharing your faith, you are missing a great blessing.

Peacemakers bring unity between men and God, and they also bring unity between men and other men. Bringing estranged people together is a blessing. Eugene Peterson, in his book *The Message*, translates Matthew 5:9 this way: "You're blessed when you can show people how to cooperate instead of to compete and to fight. That is when you discover who you really are and your place in God's family." That's why Jesus warned us to reconcile with other people before coming to worship Him. We need to be at peace with men to really experience the blessing of peace with God. Whether or not we are the ones at fault, we are called by God to make peace before we can truly worship Him. Happy is the man who helps put things back together.

Where Are Peacemakers Found?

If you look back over the Beatitudes, you'll find a very simple but logical order to them. The first four deal with some of the negative things we are not to be:

Happiness comes to the man who is not self-sufficient but is humble.

Happiness comes to the man who is not self-satisfied but is hurting.

Happiness comes to the man who is not self-important but harnessed.

Happiness comes to the man who is not self-satisfied but hungry for God.

The next three Beatitudes tell us what we are to be:

Those who have received mercy will be merciful.
Those who have been made pure will be pure.
Those who have received peace will be peacemakers.

I believe the Lord gave these in a very specific order, for they fit together as couplets. Poverty of spirit causes one to mourn.

Meekness causes one to be hungry for God. Mercy toward men is born out of a pure heart. With that sort of order in mind, consider how being a peacemaker is linked to the next Beatitude, being persecuted. Where are peacemakers found? In war zones. Persecution means taking the heat for what we believe, and in that environment we need peacemakers. If Christians are going to be under attack, there is a need for peacemakers.

With all the unhappiness and violence in American homes, we need peacemakers. I believe many Christian counselors are serving exactly that function, bringing peace to a troubled family. Too many Christian marriages are falling apart, and we need godly men and women who can sit down with couples and help them reconcile and find peace. We need peacemakers in our communities, bringing reconciliation between races. We need peacemakers in the international community, bringing peace to warring nations. We even need peacemakers in the Church, bringing reconciliation between churches and denominations, and sometimes even among church members. I've seen people get into serious disputes over the church organ, the carpet, the elders, the choir, and the pastor. Billy Graham has noted that Mary and Joseph lost the young boy Jesus in church one day, and in the same way too many Christians have lost Jesus in the church. They've become so busy arguing about church stuff that they've lost Christ in the process. "As much as depends on you," Paul tells the Roman Christians, "live peaceably with all men" (Romans 12:18). In other words, if there isn't a moral issue of doctrinal dispute, be a peacemaker, not a war-monger.

I read about two deacons who had been quarreling over an old fence that lay between their houses. They argued so much the two men eventually stopped talking to one another. But then one of them, wanting to make peace, brought his Bible to that fence and asked his brother to read it while he prayed. "I can't read," the man said, "I forgot my glasses." So the first man suggested, "Here, use mine." As they read the Bible and prayed together, those two men found peace. As the one man handed back the other's glasses, he said, "You know, that old fence really looks different through your glasses." That's exactly what a peacemaker does. He sees through the eyes of the other person to bring them together. When we have peace with God, we can learn to see things from God's perspective and become a peacemaker.

When the walls of communism fell in that wonderful summer of 1989, the church was at the core of the peacemaking. As the tanks of Poland, Hungary, East Germany, Czechoslovakia, Bulgaria, Romania, Russia, and Yugoslavia rolled into the cities, they were met by crowds of people on their knees, praying. Half a billion people threw off the yoke of oppression with very little violence. The Christians led the way as peacemakers, praying and singing songs, and the lie that was communism came to an end. The joy and excitement that filled the people was a wonder to behold, as decades of war came to an end. The peacemakers reflect the peace of God to the world. It's obvious to everyone. "Blessed are the peacemakers, for they shall be called sons of God."

APPLICATION

---

1. With all man's desire for peace, why do you think there is so little peace in our world?

How does the world situation mirror the lack of peace in many homes?

2. What does it mean to have peace with God?

Where does that peace come from?

How is that different from having the peace of God?

Do you have the peace of God in your life?

3. What do the following passages teach us about peace?

John 14:27

John 16:33

Romans 5:1

Romans 8:6

Romans 12:18

1 Corinthians 7:15

Ephesians 2:14

Colossians 3:15

1 Thessalonians 5:13

Hebrews 12:14

4. How is a Christian a peacemaker between men and God?

How are we to be peacemakers between men?

How does becoming a peacemaker set us apart from the rest of the world?

5. What is the pattern of peacemaking in Matthew 5:23-24?

Who is responsible to make peace if you have wronged another?

Who is responsible if you have been wronged?

6. Where does our world need peace now?

Are there people with whom you must make peace?

Make a list of the people with whom you can begin to reach out and become a peacemaker. Then pray through that list, asking God to give you an opportunity.

DID YOU KNOW?

Colossians 3:15 encourages us to let the peace of God "rule" in our hearts. The word *rule* is actually the term we use as "umpire." In other words, the peace of God ought to be the umpire of our lives, helping us know the right things to do and calling into question the mistakes we make.

HAPPY ARE THE HARASSED

Matthew 5:10-12

This chapter will examine the last of the Beatitudes.

OUTLINE

Christians who take a stand for God can expect to be persecuted. Throughout history, those who have represented Christ have suffered persecution. But there is great joy to be found in knowing that your persecution identifies you with the Lord.

I. **The Reason for Persecution**
II. **The Rewards for Persecution**
   A. Persecution Is a Compliment
   B. Persecution Identifies You with Christ
   C. Persecution Is a Catalyst
   D. Persecution Is a Criteria

OVERVIEW

lessed are those who are persecuted for righteousness' sake, for theirs is the kingdom of heaven. Blessed are you when they revile and persecute you, and say all kinds of evil against you falsely for My sake. Rejoice and be exceedingly glad, for great is your reward in heaven, for so they persecuted the prophets who were before you" (Matthew 5:10-12).

Jenny Adams serves in Peru as a missionary with Baptist Mid-Missions. She has been there for 34 years, ministering faithfully as a teacher at the mission's Bible school and in several remote villages. She drove her own van and often gave passengers rides into town. One day she offered a ride to a young woman who had previously attended the mission school, the daughter of a village pastor. Little did Miss Adams know that this young woman's brother was a cocaine processor who frequently used his sister to transport the drugs. Miss Adams was arrested with more than 3 kilos of cocaine in her vehicle, and under Peruvian law a person is guilty until proven innocent. In her case, the press was quick to exploit the story to discredit foreign missionaries. The newspapers dubbed her "the cocaine missionary," and her long years of service were ignored. After 20 days of imprisonment, Jenny Adams was released, but not until the work of her mission had suffered from false witnesses. She was innocent of all charges, but that didn't matter. She was persecuted anyway.

Nobody wants to be persecuted, and it doesn't seem natural to find happiness in persecution. Everybody I know wants to be liked, and wants to get along with others, so it's really hard to understand how anyone could find blessing in being persecuted. As a matter of fact, it seems like Christians should be complimented for their extraordinary behavior, not vilified for their faith. It would seem reasonable to think that others would respect our lifestyle, even if they didn't agree with it. Yet in this world, that's not how it happens. Good people are persecuted in this life.

Second Timothy 3:12 says, "Yes, and all who desire to live godly in Christ Jesus will suffer persecution." We ought to expect persecution. Christ was persecuted, and so were His disciples. They turned the world upside down everywhere they went, causing an uproar because their values and faith were in complete contradiction to a world lost in sin. Everyone who tries to live for Jesus in this world can expect opposition.

The Reason for Persecution

The kind of persecution we're talking about is that which occurs "for righteousness' sake," the kind that comes from having your life identified with Jesus Christ. We shouldn't assume that everything bad that happens to us is persecution. Sometimes our own stress, sin, or bad choices can bring difficulties into our lives. First Peter 4:15 reads, "Let none of you suffer as a murderer, a thief, an evildoer, or as a busybody in other people's matters." We can get into a lot of trouble just by doing the wrong things, but that doesn't make it persecution. If we are in trouble for doing something wrong, we have no business taking the blessing of Matthew 5:10 to heart.

To be persecuted for righteousness' sake means that we are hated or opposed solely for being a follower of Christ. When we are doing what is right and living for God, yet suffer because of it, that is persecution. Some feel it on the job, some are faced with it in school, and some of us have run into it in social and civic situations. This world belongs to Satan, is at war with God, and attacks Christians because they represent God in this world. We become the social conscience of the environment in which we live. Sometimes we don't have to say a thing; we can just walk around and be different. People don't like those who are different; they want us to be like them.

When I was a student in seminary, I worked for the Illinois California Express as a dock hand. I worked from 3 until 8 every day loading freight trucks and lacing tires. I'd throw tires up into the truck and then lace them so they'd stay put. It was the dirtiest job in the business, but I worked with some guys who came in white T-shirts and never got them sweaty or soiled. That was no way for a Christian to work, so I ignored them and simply started throwing tires left and right. I had rubber all over my clothes, sweat pouring down my face, and tires all around me. Then one day the union steward came down to my end of the dock and said, "Son, you've got to quit what you're doing." When I asked him what he meant, he said to me, "You can't work like you're working. You're showing us up. You'd better quit or you're going to have a lot of trouble here."

Now I was just putting in an honest day's work, and I discovered that if you work hard, the time goes faster. I didn't want to spend my day sitting around trying to figure out how to get my job done! So I did my job with all my heart. I didn't say anything or offer any words of criticism to the others, I just worked the way I thought was honoring to God. But I found out about persecution. Nobody would sit with me in the lunch room. No one would talk with me on the job. I was persecuted for righteousness' sake.

Jesus describes how that will occur by using three different words. First, He says you will be *reviled*. That word literally means to throw things into your face. For example, when Christ was hanging on the cross, some of those in attendance made fun of him, mocking him with vile, malicious words. We can't just expect to be chased out of the groups of which we are a part; we will also be subject to evil words and scorn. People will say bad things about us, just as they did about Christ. If we live for Jesus, we can't expect that non-Christians are going to understand us or accept us.

The second term Christ uses is *persecute*—they will *persecute* you. In other words, they will come after us because we are good and they are evil, and evil hates good. Persecution has been around since the fall of man. Cain killed Abel because his own works were evil but his brother's righteous. Joseph was persecuted because his father loved him. Moses was reviled, Samuel rejected, Elijah despised, and Nehemiah oppressed. Jesus Christ, the faithful witness of His Father, was put to death by the people to whom He came to minister. Stephen was stoned for speaking the truth, John and Peter were cast in prison, and James was beheaded for preaching the Good News of the Kingdom. Every one of the Apostles was martyred for his faith, except for John, who was exiled to the Isle of Patmos. Why did God's people suffer such persecution? Because they were doing right.

Where did we ever get the idea that things will work out just fine if we do everything right? The Bible says exactly the opposite. I still remember the day my teenage son came up to me and said, "Dad, I just learned something. Life isn't fair." What a hard but wonderful truth. God never said life would be fair.

The third phrase Jesus used to describe the harassment of His people was that people would *"say all kinds of evil against you falsely."* Have you ever noticed how creative people can get when they're trying to make up lies about Christians? Modern entertainment seems to go out of its way to portray pastors and Christians in the ugliest way possible. Even in the Church I've marvelled at the creative ability some have to say mean things. I once told a story on my radio program about helping my son put toilet paper on someone's house because she had been terrorizing us for three weeks. Within days I received a three-page letter from somebody telling me what a bad guy I was for pushing that idea, and how we could have used the money that bought the toilet paper to help missionaries, and how he had met with the staff at his church and warned them never to do anything like toilet-papering a house! I encouraged the man to lighten up. Life is serious enough without spending our time trying to make someone else's life miserable.

The Rewards for Persecution

As Christians, we've got to expect persecution. If we live for God in this world, it will come. We don't always have control over our situation, but we do have control over our response to it. We can't determine what action will occur, but we can determine what our attitude will be. Christ says that our attitude should be one of happiness. We are to rejoice in persecution. We're to be exceedingly glad. That may sound like it doesn't make sense, but the fact is persecution brings rewards in which we can rejoice.

Persecution Is a Compliment

To persecute someone is to show that you take him so seriously that you believe he needs to be eliminated. No one persecutes an ineffective individual. Persecution only comes to the person whose life is so positive and effective that our fallen world considers him dangerous. George Bernard Shaw once said that the finest compliment the world can pay an author is to burn his books. Those books must be powerful to raise the hackles of the world.

I once saw a film about a football player whose coach was always on him. Every time he turned around, the coach was barking at him about something. When the player finally complained, the coach told him, "Son, thank the Lord I'm after you. I don't have any plans for all those other guys I don't yell at. But I'm on your case because you've got potential. And I'm going to stay on your case until you fulfill the potential I see in you." Persecution is a compliment. It's a way of showing us that we're being effective, that we've attracted the attention of Satan, that what we're doing is so powerful the enemy wants to eliminate us.

Persecution Identifies You with Christ

When we are persecuted for righteousness' sake, it is proof that we're on the right side. Christ once told His disciples, "You will be hated by all for My name's sake. But he who endures to the end will be saved" (Matthew 10:22). Jesus Christ is a King in exile. We who are His followers are identified with Him and looked down upon because we are like Him. The Lord was persecuted by a world that didn't understand Him, and as His followers we can expect the same persecution.

Matthew tells us that the prophets got this same treatment. Throughout history, everyone who has been unafraid to stand up and be counted for Christ has taken flak. It is a witness that we are living for Christ in a world that doesn't know Him.

I preach every Sunday, and I love to talk about the good and positive things in the Bible. But the Word of God also has some hard things to say. When I come across those hard things, I will often think to myself, "Lord, do I really need to preach that?! I'd rather not." But I do, since the Bible is God's revelation to us. And when I preach those hard things, I invariably get notes from people who don't like hearing them. Sometimes people will leave the service because they don't like what is being said. I've been criticized for being too clear about the truth. But what option do I have? I can either preach the whole truth and be obedient to God, or I can compromise and make everybody comfortable. God hasn't called me to preach only the "nice" parts of Scripture but the entire message of God.

We all face moments like that. Perhaps it's at a business meeting when they bring out the glasses and call for a round of drinks. Your response to your client might make a difference in whether or not you get the deal. You have to make a decision, and it could cost you the client. But to participate in something you believe to be wrong can cost you your clear conscience and the Lord's blessing on your life. When you are persecuted, you are identified with Jesus Christ.

Persecution Is a Catalyst

The Bible says that when we suffer for righteousness, we experience growth. The best lessons are the ones we learn in hard times. Most of us really don't learn very well from prosperity and good times. I've learned my most valuable lessons and grown the most in my walk with Christ when I have experienced pain and difficulties. "We also glory in tribulations," Paul says in Romans 5:3-5, "knowing that tribulation produces perseverance; and perseverance, character; and character, hope. Now hope does not disappoint, because the love of God has been poured out in our hearts by the Holy Spirit who was given to us."

Nobody enjoys going through hard times, but we always look back and know that it was those difficulties that caused us to grow. If you are having stress at work or at school, and you are trying to do right, keep track of what God is teaching you in the process. Don't forget those lessons, for the Lord is shaping you into a more mature Christian, building Christlikeness into your life.

Persecution Is a Criteria

Jesus tells us to rejoice in persecution, for "great is your reward in heaven." Persecution is a condition, a criteria for something better God has in store for those who love Him. "If indeed we suffer with Him," it says in Romans 8:17, "that we may also be glorified together." To suffer persecution is to be an eventual partaker of joy.

"If we endure," Paul told Timothy, "we shall also reign with Him" (2 Timothy 2:12). There is something involved in persecution that identifies us with Jesus Christ and is the criteria for blessing here on earth and in eternity. In the process of being God's person, we start to find persecution happening to us. Remember that the persecuted are happy because they are being prepared for heaven.

Persecution is one of the natural consequences of living the Christian life. It is to the Christian what growing pains are to a child. No persecution, no reward. No suffering, no glory. No struggle, no victory. First Peter 5:10 asks that the God of all grace "who called us to His eternal glory by Christ Jesus, after you have suffered a while, perfect, establish, strengthen, and settle you." God wants to make a difference in our world through your life.

APPLICATION

1. In your view, are Christians being harassed in our country?

What makes you say that? In what ways are they harassed?

Why do Christians suffer persecution in this world?

2. What does it mean to suffer "for righteousness' sake"?

Have you ever suffered persecution when it wasn't for righteousness' sake?

Have you ever been persecuted for your faith? How did it happen?

3. What do these passages have to say about persecution:

Matthew 10:22

Romans 5:3-5

2 Timothy 3:12

Hebrews 11:35-40

1 Peter 5:10

4. How can persecution be seen as a compliment?

How does persecution identify you with Christ?

In what ways is persecution a catalyst for spiritual growth?

Has your persecution caused you to walk closer to the Lord?

5. What can we learn about persecution from reading Hebrews 11?

What does that chapter suggest that we can expect as God's ambassadors on earth?

6. What promise does 2 Timothy 2:12 make regarding persecution?

What does Romans 8:17 add regarding that promise?

Take the time to write a prayer to the Lord regarding persecution. Ask Him to make you strong in the face of persecution, so you can reveal your faith and trust in Him.

DID YOU KNOW?

The word *persecute* is the same root word from which we get "pursue." It means to hunt something down, to chase after it. Before his conversion Paul persecuted the church, hunting down Christians and seeing to it that they were punished. As a Christian, you can expect that non-Christians will look for ways to demean you and will take pleasure in making your life hard.

HOW TO REALLY BE HAPPY

Matthew 5:1-12

In this final chapter, we will explore the biblical prescription for happiness.

OUTLINE

E veryone is looking for happiness in our world, but few find it. Those who set big goals and achieve them often find that success doesn't bring the happiness it promised. True joy is not found in worldly success but in worshipping God.

I. How to Be Happy
   A. Understand the Pull of the World on Your Life
   1. The progression of the world
   2. The pull of the world
   3. The permanence of the world
   B. Undertake an Aggressive Program in
      the Word

I read a book recently theorizing that the two greatest revolutions in this century were the communist revolution, now dead, and the Freudian revolution, now stronger than ever. Every year more than 4 billion dollars go into counseling in this country, as Americans seek to solve the riddle of their unhappiness. Psychology is no longer the province of some arcane theorizing by European intellectuals or a luxury available only to those who have enough money to buy professional consolation for their troubled egos. Nowadays everybody is either in recovery or in denial. We're all rehabilitating our psyches, getting in touch with our inner child, and joining support groups to talk about our depressions, anxieties, compulsions, neuroses, and search for self-esteem.

The fact is, what we're trying to do in this country is to find happiness. The things we thought would make us happy haven't worked, so people are heading by the thousands to counselors to find out why. It is estimated that 80 million Americans will see a counselor next year, and thousands of people will start new careers as counselors. The search for happiness has caused a boom in the counseling industry.

How to Be Happy

Not long ago, ABC television ran a special called "The Mystery of Happiness." They went to those we would normally expect to be happy to find out if achieving their dream had changed their lives. For example, they asked a woman who had won $26 million in a lottery if she was happy. "Not really," was her response. They asked European royalty and Pulitzer Prize winners if they were happy, but they weren't. They even talked with sports stars, but most of them could only talk about their dissatisfaction with their contracts. One guy, the quarterback of a Super Bowl winning team, said that after winning the big game, all he could think of was, "Is this all there is?"

I was amazed that non-Christians put this together, since the entire program pointed out the unhappiness of man. About all they could do was reveal how babies get happy when they get what they want and become unhappy when we take things away. But anybody can find out what God says will make mankind happy—just read Matthew chapter five. Jesus says to us that we won't find happiness in the things of the world. We can devote our lives to pleasure, accomplishment, fame, money, or anything else that the world values and promotes, but they won't make us happy. Instead, Christ offers a series of startling messages on how to be happy, stating things in complete opposition to what the world says will make us happy.

Happy are the humble. The world tells us not to be humble. We need to be self-assertive, make sure everybody knows how good we are, and tell our story. The world suggests we even brag a little, so that we'll get noticed. But Jesus says that it will be the humble who inherit the kingdom of heaven. God will resist the proud and exalt the humble. He will draw near to those who have a recognition that they are incomplete apart from God.

Happy are the hurting. The world says to avoid pain at all costs. Whatever we have to do to get rid of mourning, we should do it. Cover it up, ignore it, mask it, or pretend it's not there, because we want to stay away from pain. But Jesus says that the most profound experiences we ever have will come from pain. The greatest truths will be learned through suffering. Some of our most joyous moments will be when everything on the outside is dictating anguish in our lives. Happy are those who hurt, for they shall be comforted.

Happy are the harnessed. The world says that we can have it all. If we've got power, we ought to use it. Take every resource to the limit and grab for all the gusto we can. But Jesus says that real happiness is when your power is controlled by the Spirit of God. Joy comes in knowing we have power, but it is under control. We don't have to demonstrate power continually, regardless of the world's expectations.

Happy are the hungry. The world says that we don't want to be hungry; we want to be satisfied. We don't want to have anything lacking in our lives, since that's a sign of not being successful, so we need to get everything we can. We should gorge ourselves on things. We should drive ourselves to be successful in today's world. But Jesus says that true joy can never be found in material things. Happiness comes from having an inner desire to know God and to want to partake of His nature. Those people who fill themselves up on the Lord, rather than the world, will find real happiness.

Happy are the helpers. The world says that happiness is being served by others. The world is a triangle, and when we get to the top everyone below us will serve us. So we should do everything in our power to get above others. But Jesus says that He came into this world not to be served but to serve. He came to give His life away. Happiness is found in serving others, not in being served. If you want to be great in God's kingdom, learn to be the servant of all. Happy are those who are merciful to others, for they shall be ministered to.

Happy are the holy. The world says that joy is found in unrestrained freedom. Sex, drugs, and any pleasurable experience are lifted up as the ultimate goal and glorified as hallmarks of "freedom." Perversions are marched down Main Street in the name of free speech. This is supposed to give us a sense that we control our own destiny, that we can make our existence happy through the indulgence of sinful delights. But Jesus says that holy people are the ones who are truly happy. I've been a pastor for more than thirty years, and I've yet to meet a happy adulterer. We don't find joy through unrestrained passion. Happiness comes from having a clean heart and knowing that we are walking close to the Almighty.

Happy are the healers. The world says that we are in competition with our fellow workers and should build competitions, use politics, beat people, knock each other out and climb over the carnage to get to the top. But Jesus says that the happy people are the peacemakers, those who can heal situations rather than exacerbate them. Find people who are hurting and heal them. If you've got a problem with a colleague, mend it. Rather than dividing people, unite them. Happiness is found not in creating war but in establishing peace.

Happy are the harassed. The world wants us to conform to its image. It wants us to live by its standards. It is at war with God, and expects us to be, too. If we decide to stand with God, they'll attack us. They'll say bad things about us, harass us, and try to ruin our reputations. But Jesus says we ought to be happy when persecution comes, for it is a sign that we belong to God. We can be happy in the face of harassment, for we know that our lives must be making an impact or the devil wouldn't bother with us.

As I look over Christ's design for happiness, I'm struck by the fact that it isn't the list I would have created. This wouldn't be the formula for happiness that I would have suggested. But these are exactly the things that will bring happiness. The world is in direct opposition to God, so God's formula for success is directly opposite to the world's. We can have the blessing and benediction of God if we'll follow these principles.

Understand the Pull of the World on Your Life

The Christian life isn't easy. Just knowing the Beatitudes will not make us happy. We live in this world, but we aren't of the world. So while we're living in this culture, we have to learn how to live God's way, and that will create tension with our world. Psalm 1 helps describe how we can do this: "Blessed is the man who walks not in the counsel of the ungodly, nor stands in the path of sinners, nor sits in the seat of the scornful" (v. 1). There are three things to notice in that verse.

The progression of the world. There are people in this world who are ungodly; that is, they live life without God. They aren't going in any direction; they simply don't have God in their lives. The next step away from God is toward sin, and the psalmist says that there are people in the world who are sinners, overtly acting in opposition to God's truth. The third sort of people are the scornful, those who are rebellious against God and blasphemous in their attitude toward Him. As a person is pulled into the world, he is pulled away from God and toward sin and rebellion.

The pull of the world. Notice that the writer uses three words to describe the world's pull on us. First he talks about those who listen to the counsel of the ungodly, getting information from those who have no knowledge of God. Second, he speaks of the path of sinners, which is when we start following a path away from God. Third, he tells of the seat of sinners—those who have grown completely comfortable in their lives apart from God. If a man will look back over his life, he'll find that the things with which he used to be uncomfortable have gradually become comfortable to him. That's the pull of the world.

The permanence of the world. The author of the psalm says we first walk, or associate, with those separated from God. Then we stand with sinners, identifying ourselves with them. Finally we sit with the scoffers, making their lifestyle our own. This is the pattern of our world, and it's sucking Christians into it every day. Jesus stepped into this system and said, "I don't want My people to live like that in the world. Here is God's alternative." Then He explained how we can find happiness. By living out the Beatitudes, we can experience the life-changing power of God in the midst of an evil culture.

Undertake an Aggressive Program in the Word

The only way to survive in a world which tries to slowly poison our minds is to renew our minds each day. The psalmist says in Psalm 1 that the blessed man is the one who delights in the law of the Lord, meditating on it day and night. When I open my Bible for personal devotions, I know that I'm looking at the very Word of God. It's different from everything else around me. What I'm reading is in a whole different universe. I'm getting a transfusion of heavenly culture into my system. I know that if I try to make it in this world, I'll get pulled down. I'll never be happy following the world's plan.

But when I came to Jesus Christ, the happiness of this world was ruined for me. I've got the Holy Spirit inside me, and I can never be happy unless I'm walking with Him. People can try to be happy, but they'll never achieve it apart from the Lord. Christians can try to follow the world's plan for happiness, but the only way to find it is to let the Word of God cleanse and renew them.

Paul said to the Christians in Rome, "I beseech you therefore, brethren, by the mercies of God, that you present your bodies a living sacrifice, holy, acceptable to God, which is your reasonable service. And do not be conformed to this world, but be trans-formed by the renewing of your mind" (Romans 12:1-2). By allowing God's Word to refresh and transform you, you can begin to see the principles of Jesus Christ start to work in your life. You'll be blessed—happy. There is a path to happiness the world knows nothing about. If we spend our lives cultivating the Word of God, we'll find real happiness.

1. In your own words, why aren't there more happy people in this world?

What happens when someone realizes a dream and it still doesn't make him happy?

Do you find that getting what you want makes you happy? Does your happiness last?

2. Why do you suppose there has been such a counseling boom in this country recently?

What do people hope to get from a counselor?

3. What does the world think of humility?

Why does Christ say that the humble will be happy?

4. What does the world try to do with hurting?

How can Christ claim that the hurting will be happy?

5. What is the world's response to Christ's call for meekness?

In your own words, how will meekness lead to happiness?

6. What does the world promote as the sources of happiness and fulfillment?

What does Christ offer as God's alternative in Matthew 5:6?

7. Jesus claims that happiness is found in serving others, not in being served. How have you found that to be true?

How does the world respond to Christ's call to service?

8. In your own experience, are those who engage in ungodly behaviors really happy? Why or why not?

Why is becoming a peacemaker at odds with the values of this world?

9. How do you fight against the aggressive pull of the world?

What has been the best insight you've had through this study?

The word *blessed* is actually *eulogia* in the Greek. We get the word *eulogy* from it, the message that is preached at a person's funeral service. A eulogy is a nice way of summing up all the good things that person has done and the positive impact they left on the world. For the Christian, our lives are to be a eulogy, blessing those with whom we come in contact and creating joy in the lives of others. That's what Christ has called us to in the world.

Turning Point
Resource Books
By Dr. David Jeremiah

What the Bible Says About Angels
Dr. Jeremiah goes straight to God's Word to deliver fascinating insights about angels, God's majestic messengers. You'll learn that the Bible's rich teaching on angels is not a trivial fad but a fascinating doorway into sound, life-giving, spiritual truth that will help you draw closer than ever to the God you serve.
ANGHBK (Hardback) **$19**
ANGSG (Study Guide) **$9**

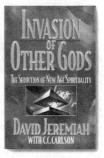

Invasion of Other Gods:
The Seduction of New Age Spirituality
Every day you and your family are bombarded with consciousness-raising programs, techniques for self-improvement, and innovative spiritual practices—all influenced by the "New Spirituality." Can you discern between modern trends and ancient paganism? Authors David Jeremiah and Carole Carlson warn us that the two can be identical.
IOGHBK (Hardback) **$18**
IOGSG (Study Guide) **$9**

Escape the Coming Night:
The Bright Hope of Revelation
Let Dr. David Jeremiah be your guide through the terrifying heights and unfathomable depths of the Book of Revelation. Arm yourself with prophetic truth about things to come so you can live every moment for God, because the end is so near.
REVBK $10
REVSGP (Study Guide pkg., 4 volumes) **$28**

The Handwriting on the Wall:
Secrets from the Prophecies of Daniel
Daniel, divinely inspired, accurately prophesied the rise and fall of empires and their rulers. We cannot pass Daniel off as just the man in the lion's den or the "dreamer." To know Daniel is to know how to live today and look into the future with confidence.
HOWBK $12
HOWSGP (Study Guide pkg., 3 volumes) **$22**

ORDER 1-800-947-1993

OTHER STUDY GUIDES & BOOKS
AVAILABLE THROUGH TURNING POINT

Audio cassette albums are also available. For information use our toll-free number.

SELECTION	CODE	QTY	PRICE	TOTAL
STUDY GUIDES				
Escape the Coming Night (Revelation, 4 volume package)	REVSGP	___	$ 28	$ ___
Acts of Love: The Power of Encouragement	AOLSG	___	$ 9	___
For Such a Time As This—The Book of Esther	ESTSG	___	$ 9	___
Ten Burning Questions from Psalms	TBQSG	___	$ 9	___
Knowing the God You Worship	KGWSG	___	$ 9	___
Seeking Wisdom—Finding Gold	WISSG	___	$ 9	___
The Handwriting on the Wall (Daniel, 3 volume pkg.)	HOWSGP	___	$ 22	___
Invasion of Other Gods (New Age)	IOGSG	___	$ 9	___
Worship	WORSG	___	$ 9	___
Turning Toward Integrity (James)	TTIBK	___	$ 10	___
Turning Toward Joy (Philippians)	TTJBK	___	$ 10	___
The Power of Love (1 Corinthians 13)	POLSG	___	$ 9	___
Spiritual Warfare (Ephesians 6)	SPWSG	___	$ 9	___
The Fruit of the Spirit (Galatians 5:16-26)	FOSSG	___	$ 9	___
Home Improvement	HMISG	___	$ 9	___
What the Bible Says About Angels	ANGSG	___	$ 9	___
Greatest Stories Ever Told (Parables)	GSTSG	___	$ 9	___
A Nation in Crisis (Joshua, Volume 1)	NICSG1	___	$ 9	___
A Nation in Crisis (Joshua, Volume 2)	NICSG2	___	$ 9	___
When Wisdom Turns to Foolishness (Solomon)	WTFSG	___	$ 9	___
Signs of the Second Coming (Matthew 24 & 25)	SSCSG	___	$ 9	___
Core Values of the Church (1 Corinthians, 3 Volume pkg.)	CVCSGP	___	$ 22	___
BOOKS				
The Handwriting on the Wall (Daniel)	HOWBK	___	$ 12	___
Escape the Coming Night (Revelation)	REVBK	___	$ 10	___
Acts of Love: The Power of Encouragement	AOLHBK	___	$ 18	___
Overcoming Loneliness	OCLBK	___	$ 10	___
Invasion of Other Gods (New Age)	IOGHBK	___	$ 18	___
What the Bible Says About Angels	ANGHBK	___	$ 19	___

For information and Discover, Visa, or MasterCard orders call:

1-800-947-1993

POSTAGE AND HANDLING CHART

For Orders	Add
Up to $5.99	$1.50
$6.00-$19.99	$2.50
$20.00-$50.99	$3.50
$51.00-$99.99	$6.00
$100.00 & over	$9.00

MERCHANDISE TOTAL	___
SHIPPING/HANDLING	___
SUBTOTAL	___
CA RESIDENTS ONLY ADD 7.25% TAX	___
GIFT TO MINISTRY	___
TOTAL	$ ___

Please enclose payment with order. Make check or money order payable to:

TURNING POINT • P.O. Box 3838 • San Diego, CA 92163-1838 *(Please allow 4-6 weeks for delivery.)*

Mr/Mrs/Miss _____

Address _____

City/State/Zip _____

I listen to *Turning Point* on (station call letters): _____ Phone _____